of the MOUNTAINS & VALLEYS

T. Ernest Wilson

Books by T. Ernest Wilson

Angola Beloved

The Farewell Ministry of Christ

God's Call to Special Service

The Messianic Psalms

Mystery Doctrines of the New Testament

1 Thessalonians (*What the Bible Teaches* Series)

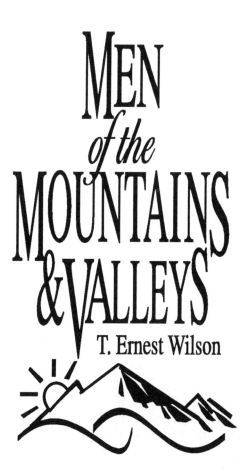

MEN
of the
MOUNTAINS
&VALLEYS

T. Ernest Wilson

GOSPEL FOLIO PRESS
P. O. Box 2041, Grand Rapids MI 49501-2041
Available in the UK from
JOHN RITCHIE LTD., Kilmarnock, Scotland

Cover design and photo by J. B. Nicholson, Jr.

Published by Gospel Folio Press
P. O. Box 2041, Grand Rapids MI 49501-2041

ISBN 1-882701-00-3

Printed in the United States of America

There's a light upon the mountains,
And the day is at the spring,
When our eyes shall see the beauty
And the glory of the King;
Weary was our heart with waiting,
And the night-watch seemed so long,
But His triumph-day is breaking,
And we hail it with a song.
—Henry Burton

Contents

Part One
Introduction

The highest mountain in the world is Mount Everest, at 29,028 feet, a peak of the Himalayas, on the border between Nepal and Tibet. The expedition which first reached its summit in 1953 was the eighth to make the attempt. The leader was Col. John Hunt of Great Britain. After careful planning and incredible hardships and dangers, two gallant members of the expedition, Edmund P. Hillary, a New Zealand beekeeper, and Tenzing Norgay, a Sherpa guide and veteran mountaineer, stood on the summit of the world. It was 11:30 AM on May 29, 1953. Hillary described his feelings:

"My initial feelings were of relief—relief that there were no more steps to cut, no more ridges, and no more humps to tantalize us with hopes of success. I looked at Tenzing and in spite of his balaclava, goggles, and oxygen mask all encrusted with long icicles that concealed his face, there was no disguising his infectuous grin of pure delight as he looked all around him. The ridge had taken us two and a half hours, but it seemed like a lifetime. I turned off the oxygen and removed my set. I had carried my camera loaded with color film inside my shirt to keep it warm, so I now produced it and got Tenzing to pose on top for me, waving his axe on which was a string of flags—United Nations, British, Nepalese and Indian. Then I turned my attention to the great stretch of country lying below me in every direction.

To the East was our giant neighbor Makalu, unexplored and unclimbed, and even on top of Everest the mountaineering instinct was sufficiently strong to spend some moments conjecturing as to whether a route up that mountain might not exist. Far away across the clouds, the great bulk of Kangchenjunga loomed on the horizon. To the west, Cho Oyu, our old adversary of 1952 dominated the scene, and we could see the great, unexplored ranges of Nepal stretching off into the distance."

The *Encyclopedia Britanica*, in its article on Everest, asks the question, "Why do men climb mountains?" and suggests an answer given by Rudyard Kipling:

> *Something hidden, go and find it,*
> *Go and look behind the Ranges,*
> *Something lost behind the Ranges,*
> *Lost and waiting for you, Go!*

But the Bible has the real answer. It has a lot to say about mountains and the men associated with them. It is important to recognize that every mountain has a corresponding valley. The one balances the other. Life is like that—it has its ups and downs. It may be true to say that in the life of every true Christian there is a mountaintop experience. It may be short, but it is very precious and is never forgotten. Very few, if any, of God's men are on the mountain all the time. God is not only the God of the mountaintop but of the valley as well (see 1 Kings 20:28). This little volume is an attempt to outline some of the great men of Holy Scripture and their experiences on the mountain and in the valley. Associated with this are many great truths that have relevance for the present day.

In Scripture, the mountaintop is a place of revelation, a lonely place, a dangerous place, often covered with eternal snow and rarified air. It is no place for weaklings or cowards.

In the Old Testament there are six outstanding men associated with a mountain. They are: Noah and Mount Ararat (Gen. 6-9); Abraham and Mount Moriah (Gen. 22; 2 Chron. 3); Moses and Mount Sinai (Ex. 19-40); Caleb and Mount Hebron (Josh. 14; Jud. 1:10-15); David and Mount Zion (2 Sam. 5:6-10); Elijah and Mount Carmel (1 Ki. 18).

The first book in the New Testament, Matthew, records seven scenes of Christ on a mountain at critical points in His earthly ministry, with important teaching connected with each one. These are: the Mount of Temptation (Matt. 4:1-11); the Mount of Teaching (chs. 5-7); the Mount of Intercession (ch. 14:23-33); the Mount of Transfiguration (ch. 17:1-9); the Mount of Olives—His Coming (chs. 24-25); and Mount Calvary—His Crucifixion (ch. 27); the Mountain in Galilee—His Commission (ch. 28:16-20).

The last book in the New Testament, Revelation, ends with the last survivor of the Apostolic witnesses, the venerable John, being carried away in the Spirit to a great and high mountain to see the great city, the Holy Jerusalem descending out of heaven from God, having the glory of God, the Bride, the Lamb's wife. It is the peak, the culminating point of mountaintop experiences in the Bible.

1
Noah & Mount Ararat

The Age Before the Flood

From Adam to the Flood was a period of approximately 1600 years. Man had been commanded to multiply, to subdue the earth and have dominion over every living thing (Gen. 1:28). Alas, sin intervened and as a result of the Fall, the original mandate for dominion was lost. But in spite of this, there must have been a considerable population increase (Gen. 6:1).

Genesis 4 and 5 describe two distinct kinds of people and life-styles that are traced to the seventh generation. Genesis 4 describes "The way of Cain" (Jude 11). It commences with a murder and reaches its climax in a song or ditty boasting of another murder. Lamech, its author, is the first recorded polygamist. Marriage, instituted by God, and the principles concerning it were arrogantly ignored. The Cainite civilization was characterized by urban development, cattle ranching, musical entertainment, and heavy industry (vv. 17-22). Cain, like Judas many centuries later, went out from the presence of the Lord (v. 16), and is the prototype of apostasy and departure from God.

On the other hand, chapter 5 traces the line of godly Seth, characterized by faith, and reaches its climax in the seventh generation in another Lamech, the father of Noah. Two names are prominent in the line of Seth, those of Enoch and Methuselah. Enoch walked with God, pleased God, and was translated by God before judgment fell. Methuselah lived longer than any other—969 years. His name means: "When he is dead, it shall be sent." When he died, the Flood came. Enoch must have been divinely inspired in naming his son.

Chapter 6 gives a graphic account of the condition of mankind in the period immediately before the Flood. That age commenced with a satanic attack in the Garden of Eden, with the Fall and its dreadful consequences. It ends with another diabolical attack with equally devastating results.

There are a number of allusions in the Bible to the spiritual character of this period. In Job 22:15-17, we read: "Hast thou marked the old way which wicked men have trodden? Which were cut down out of time, whose foundation was overthrown with a flood; which said unto God, Depart from us; and what can the Almighty do for them!"

Our Lord said, "But as the days of Noah were, so shall also the coming of the Son of Man be. For as the days that were before the Flood, they were eating and drinking, marrying and giving in marriage until the day that Noah entered into the ark, and knew not until the Flood came and took them all away; so shall also the coming of the Son of Man be" (Matt. 24:37-39). Yet through it all, God had a competent testimony. Adam lived 930 years into the period and must have had a tremendous influence on his progeny. Then there was the influence of Abel's sacrifice, the prophecies of Enoch (Jude 14-15); Noah, the preacher of righteousness, and above all the convicting power of the Spirit of God (Gen. 6:3).

What were the reasons for the terrible judgment of the Flood when a whole generation of mankind was wiped out, except for one family, and the earth itself subjected to the greatest cataclysm (Peter's word, 2 Pet. 2:5) since creation? There never has been anything like it since.

There are two interpretations to the liason between the

sons of God and the daughters of men (Gen. 6:2):

1) The breakdown of separation between the line of Seth and the ungodly progeny of Cain. Both lines were destroyed at the Flood. Only godly Noah and his family were spared.

2) A satanic attack on the human race. The sons of God (see Gen. 6:1-2; Job 1:6; 2:1; 38:7; 2 Pet. 2:4; Jude 6-7) are said to be fallen angels who left their first estate, invaded the human race, and who had intercourse with women. The result was the Nephelim, translated giants or fallen ones. There are difficulties with the meaning of the passage by both interpretations, but there does not seem to be any doubt that Satan was the instigator of the deplorable and desperate conditions that resulted in the judgment of God. It was his second, but not his last attack on the seed of the woman.

NOAH THE PREACHER OF RIGHTEOUSNESS

Genesis 6 describes how the wickedness of man in both lines of descent came to a head. It could be summarized in four words: mind, murder, marriage, and morals. The chapter gives God's diagnosis of the situation and His decision: "I will destroy man whom I have created from the face of the earth, both man and beast, and the creeping thing, and the fowls of the air; for it repenteth Me that I have made them." There was a period of grace of 120 years when God's patience waited. Then God's man is introduced. There are six character references of Noah. He found grace (the first reference to this great word in Scripture) in the eyes of the Lord (v. 8). He was just, perfect in his generations and, like Enoch, he walked with God (Heb. 11:7), which tells us that he was a man of faith. In the darkest hour of human history, God always has a man. He was warned by God of things not seen as yet. It is probable that he had never seen rain or a flood (Gen. 2:5-6). God's revelation of a coming catastrophic judgment caused him to be moved with fear. Fear is a healthy, normal feeling. The bravest men are those who act in spite of their fear. He acted in faith and in response to God's oracular warning.

When Noah was building and preaching, it was not so much what he said, but what he did that proclaimed the coming judgment. Every blow of the axe and every nail or dowel he drove home was a sermon. There would be smart witticisms from the onlookers and those that passed by. Practical men would think him a fool. But he went on hammering; he did not seem such a fool when water was to the knees of the jesters, and their sarcasms faded away as they drowned.

HE PREPARED AN ARK TO THE SAVING OF HIS HOUSE

The ark is a graphic picture of Christ as the only means of salvation. God was the designer and Noah the builder. It was made of gopher wood, probably cypress, an incorruptible wood. Taking the cubit as 18 inches, the dimensions were 450 feet long, 45 feet high, with a beam of 75 feet. The measurements represent the basic proportions in modern ship construction. Probably it did not have a pointed bow and a cruiser stern like a modern ocean liner. Likely it was a huge barge with a flat bottom, made for floating and not for speed and practically impossible to capsize. The word for "ark" is not the same as the ark of the covenant (Ex. 25:10) but is the word used for the ark of bulrushes (Ex. 2:3). It had to withstand tidal waves, wind, and the greatest storm the world had ever seen. There were four main items in the plans.

1) It was covered inside and outside with pitch. The word for "pitch" is caphar. It is the same word as "atonement" in Leviticus 17:11. The hull was completely covered, making it practically watertight.

2) It had a door in the side. No measurement is given. It had to be large enough to admit the huge elephant and the smallest rodent. There was only one door and the Lord had charge of it. It was the Lord who gave the invitation to enter and it was the Lord who shut the door (Gen. 7:1, 16).

3) There were three rooms or stories or decks, literally

"nests." There is speculation about where the living quarters for Noah and his family and the animals were located, as well as where the considerable amount of food was stowed. Noah's family would naturally be on the upper deck as the window was there. The animals must have been divinely brought to the ark. It is well-known that wild beasts and domestic animals can sense a coming storm and look for shelter. But here it was God who directed the operation.

4) There was a window. "In a cubit thou shalt finish it above." The word window is literally an opening for light and ventilation. The phraseology is difficult. Most authorities understand that this window was to consist of an opening a cubit high extending all around the ark's circumference, near the roof. Presumably there was also an overhanging parapet provided to keep out the rain and floodwater. God had charge of the door, but Noah of the window. The door would speak of safety, salvation, and security; the window of worship and communion.

"As far as we know, there was no sail, no mast, and no rudder, only God—and that was enough" (Griffith Thomas).

THE FLOOD

The universal flood was the greatest natural disaster since creation of our planet. Peter calls it a "kataklusmos" (overflowed, 2 Pet. 3:6). Noah had preached and toiled for 120 years. Then there were seven days of calm before the storm came. God gave the command: "Come thou and all thy house into the ark." There was only a step to safety (Rev. 22:17). The Lord was inside. So to speak, He said, "Come and stay beside Me." The Lord shut him in (7:16).

Two terms describe the commencement of the Flood. "The fountains of the great deep were broken up," and "the windows of heaven were opened." It came from beneath and above. One would indicate volcanic action and the other the collapse of the vapor canopy that surrounded the earth. Few

17

things are more terrifying than the combined force of wind and water. It lasted for forty days and nights, a typical period. "Every living thing in whose nostrils was the breath of life died" (7:22). The tops of the highest hills were covered. If language means anything, especially the language of Holy Scripture, the Flood was universal. Morris and Whitcomb, in their book, "The Genesis Flood," give ten reasons for believing that it covered the whole globe. Seashells on the highest mountains, and the traditions of primitive people in every part of the world testify to this fact.

Five categories of living creatures are mentioned as having perished: fowl, cattle, beasts, creeping things, and men. All that was on the dry land died. Fossils buried in the sedimentary rocks are a silent testimony to the awful judgment. The surface of the earth, and its climate, were drastically altered. The evidence of coal in the frozen Arctic, the hundreds of thousands of tropical mammoths suddenly engulfed with food in their mouths in Siberia and Alaska, the bones and remains of animals trapped in the caves of France and in the crevices of the Rock of Gibraltar all bear witness. Deserts in Africa, China and Australia that were once fertile, all show that the earth of today is different from what it was before the Flood. After the first forty days, the waters prevailed another 150 days (7:18, 24). No other biblical event is so comprehensively dated by God as is the Flood. There are repeated references to days and months and years. There are eighteen notations in all. It would appear that Noah kept a diary, noting day by day the events of the monumental catastrophe. Altogether, it covered a period of a full year of 365 days.

MOUNT ARARAT

Mount Ararat is an extinct volcano. It stands in Turkish territory overlooking the point where the frontiers of Turkey, Iran, and Soviet Armenia converge. There are two peaks, Great and Little Ararat, separated by a saddle. The dome of the former is 16,945 feet above sea level. Its heights are in the zone of perpetual snow. It is the source of the Tigris and Euphrates rivers. Local legend maintains that the remains of the ark were long visible on the mountain. The Armenians believed that God forbade anyone from reaching the top of Mount Ararat and viewing the remains of the ark. But in September, 1829, Von Parrot, a German in Russian service made the first successful ascent of the mountain. In recent times, a number of attempts have been made to find the ark, but so far with no convincing success.

The name "Ararat" is said to mean "the curse reversed" (J. B. Jackson), or "holy ground" (F. W. Grant). Genesis 8:4 tells us "the ark *rested* in the seventh month on the seventeenth day of the month, upon the mountains of Ararat." It is significant that the Lord rose from the dead on the seventeenth day of the seventh month (Nisan). For the ark and its occupants, it was a resurrection day and a day of rest. Noah's name means "rest." They had been brought safely through the stormy waters of judgment to a place of rest on resurrection ground. Peter uses it as an illustration of the meaning of believer's baptism (1 Pet. 3:20-22). But before the door was opened and they set foot on a cleansed and renewed earth, there was a prolonged waiting period in which there was the important typical incident of the sending forth of the raven and the dove. Noah opened the window (8:6) and released both birds. But the raven never came back. It went to and fro and apparently was perfectly happy among the debris of judgment and dead bodies of those who had been swept into eternity. But the dove "had no rest for the sole of her foot" and came back to the place of rest in the ark. After a period of seven days, it was sent out again and returned with an olive leaf in its mouth, plucked off a living tree—visible evidence that life had arisen from a dead and devastated world. When the dove was sent forth the third time, she did not return, but it is not said that she had found rest for the sole of her foot. Obviously she had found some place to perch, but the statement is omitted. The typical significance comes to light in Matthew 3:16. When our Lord arose from the waters of baptism, the Holy Spirit in bodily form as a dove came and abode upon Him. Here at last the Heavenly Dove has a place where the sole of its feet can rest.

The raven and the dove in the ark are birds of a different nature as to habits and food. The raven feeds on carrion and other unclean things, but the dove is clean in its character and the things it feeds upon. When first released, there was planty to attract the raven, but there was nothing for the dove. In the New Testament, the dove becomes the emblem of the Holy Spirit; the raven, a picture of the old, unregenerate nature. Every true believer has both. We must remember that the old fallen nature feeds on that which is unclean, as does the raven. Only that which is born of the Spirit is spiritual, and, like the dove, feeds on that which is clean. Recognizing this, we must be very careful as to that which feeds our minds. It has been well said that for spiritual growth we must "starve the raven and feed the dove."

There are four important items connected with Ararat:
1) An altar and a sacrifice: it is a place of worship.
2) A covenant: it heralds a new dispensation.
3) A covenant promise: no more judgment by a flood.
4) A covenant symbol: the bow in the storm cloud.

It was the Lord (Jehovah) who invited Noah into the ark: "Come thou and all thy house into the ark," and it was the Lord who shut him in (7:1, 16). Now it is God (Elohim) who commands him, "Go forth of the ark, thou, and thy wife, and thy sons, and thy sons' wives with thee." He emerges as the head of a new race, into a new world, under new conditions. It is a fresh start for mankind. His first act is worship.

AN ALTAR AND A SACRIFICE

This is the first mention of an altar and a burnt offering in

Scripture. It is the third indication of the way of approach to a Holy God. The first was in Eden when the Lord God provided coats of skin to clothe the naked, guilty pair. It was a covering, which is the root meaning of atonement, and must have involved the shedding of blood. The second was Abel's offering of the firstfruits of the flock and the fat thereof (Gen. 4:4), indicating the divine way of approach to God. But here it is a burnt offering, pointing forward to Leviticus 1. Here we discover the reason why the clean animals were taken into the ark in sevens and the unclean only in twos. In the new environment, the unclean pair could easily thrive and survive, but why the odd one in the seven clean animals? The answer is that it was required for a burnt offering sacrifice in the new order.

Noah built an altar unto *Jehovah*, the covenant-keeping God, and offered a sacrifice of every clean beast and fowl. And the Lord smelled a sweet savor, or "a savor of rest," the word apparently being a play on the meaning of Noah's name. This is the peak in Noah's career and testimony. It all pointed forward to another sacrifice, that of Calvary, where we too can find rest.

A COVENANT: A NEW DISPENSATION

The first occurrence of the word "covenant" (berith) is found in Genesis 6:18, "But with thee (Noah) will I establish My covenant." In chapter 9, it is found seven times and overall about seventy-seven times in the Old Testament. It indicates God entering into relationship with mankind, making specific promises and requiring certain responses and obedience. Some of the covenants are conditional and others unconditional. The covenant made with Noah and his posterity was unconditional (8:21-22), and everlasting (9:16).

The covenant with Noah was given before the law of Moses and has never been repealed. It inaugurated a new dispensation, a new method of God's dealings with mankind.

The first dispensation was the age of *innocence* before the Fall in Eden, when Satan and sin entered, bringing death and disaster. The second was that of *conscience,* when there was no specific law, but the Holy Spirit was working in men's hearts to convict of right and wrong. It too ended in the disaster of the Flood. In this third period, the responsibility for *human government* is placed in man's hands. Here we have a fresh start under a new head with a new code of behavior. History is the sad record of how it worked out.

Note the following features of the covenant:

1) It was based on a blood sacrifice (8:20-21).

2) The curse on the ground was lifted (8:21).

3) A promise was made of continual natural forces (8:22).

4) Human government was committed to man (9:1-6).

5) Flesh was allowed instead of only a vegetarian diet (9:3).

6) The sanctity of blood was stressed—not to be eaten (9:4).

7) Capital punishment for culpable homicide (9:6).

8) The sign of the rainbow in the storm cloud (9:13-14)

THE COVENANT PROMISE

"And I will establish my covenant with you; neither shall all flesh be cut off anymore by the waters of a flood; neither shall there be anymore a flood to destroy the earth" (Gen. 8:21 and 9:11). Earthquakes, tidal waves, local floods and many other natural disasters, are very often the voice of God speaking in judgment to man, but never again will there be anything like the Deluge covering the whole earth as in the days of Noah. The next global cleansing will be by fire and it will involve the heavenly bodies as well (2 Pet. 3:7-12).

A further gracious promise is given: "While the earth remaineth, seedtime and harvest, and cold and heat, and summer and winter, and day and night shall not cease" (Gen. 8:22). It is evident that climatic conditions are very different from what they were before the Flood (Gen. 2:5-6). But now the heavenly bodies in relation to the earth are fixed in their orbits and move with mathematical precision to give us our seasons and weather conditions. This is God's mandate for the present era.

THE COVENANT SIGN OR TOKEN

"And God said, This is the token of the covenant which I make between Me and you and every living creature that is with you, for perpetual generations. I do set My bow in the cloud, and it shall be for a token of a covenant between Me and the earth. And it shall come to pass, when I bring a cloud over the earth, that the bow shall be seen in the cloud; and I will remember my covenant, which is between Me and you and every living creature of all flesh, and the waters shall no more become a flood to destroy all flesh" (Gen. 9:12-15).

The words, "I do set My bow in the cloud," clearly infer that a rainbow had never before been seen by mankind. It would strongly support the statement in Genesis 2:5-6 that until the time of the flood, no rain had fallen on the earth, but that it had been watered by mist. The rainbow is the child of the storm and sunshine. Three things are necessary to produce it: cloud, rain, and sun. There may be a cloud without a rainbow, but there cannot be a rainbow without a cloud. There is the dark cloud of judgment but the sun is shining still. The rainbow breaks down white light into its seven prismatic colors, with violet at the one end and red at the other. On earth we can only see a segment, a fragment of the circle, but flying above and through the clouds, the airman can see the completed circle.

The rainbow is mentioned four times in Scripture. In Genesis 9, it is a reminder of God's covenanted mercy to the survivors of a world that had been destroyed by judgment. Ezekiel 1:28 describes "the appearance of the bow that is in the cloud in the day of rain, so was the appearance . . . of the glory of the Lord. And when I saw it, I fell upon my face and I heard a voice as one that spake." John the apostle, caught up

23

to heaven, sees a throne, and round the throne a rainbow like an emerald (Rev. 4:1-3). In heaven the rainbow is a complete circle. Finally, in Revelation 10:1-3, "And I saw another mighty angel come down from heaven, clothed with a cloud; and a rainbow was upon his head, and his face was as it were the sun, and his feet as pillars of fire. And he had in his hand a little book open; and he set his right foot on the sea, and his left foot on the earth. And he cried with a loud voice, as when a lion roareth; and when he cried, seven thunders uttered their voices." The mighty angel is no doubt the Angel of the Lord Jehovah, our Lord Jesus Christ coming to claim His inheritance. The four references to the rainbow are full of precious teaching concerning God's purposes and mercy.

NOAH'S SAD LAPSE

"And Noah began to be a farmer; and he planted a vineyard. And he drank of the wine, and became drunk; and he was uncovered in his tent. And Ham, the father of Canaan, saw the nakedness of his father, and told his two brethren outside. And Shem and Japheth took a garment, and laid it upon both their shoulders, and went backward, and covered the nakedness of their father; and their faces were backward, and they saw not their father's nakedness" (9:20-23).

It is a sad commentary on human nature to find a man like Noah who had been a preacher of righteousness for 120 years, who was perfect in his generations, who had received direct communications from God, and had come through the traumatic experience of the Flood unscathed, and had worshipped God with an acceptable sacrifice on the mountaintop—to find him drunk and indecently exposed in his tent. Did he not know what he was doing when he overindulged in drinking the wine, the product of his labor in the vineyard? It is the first case of drunkenness and its serious consequences in the Bible. Later on, while the Scriptures speak of the "wine that maketh glad the heart of man" (Ps. 104:15) and that it was the drink offering poured out upon the burnt offering (Num. 15:5, 7, 10), they also warn of the sin of over-indulgence. The case of Lot and the action of his dissolute daughters is a prime example (Gen. 19:32-34).

After the untimely deaths of Nadab and Abihu, the sons of Aaron, who were smitten as they attempted to go into the sanctuary with strange fire, the Lord gave the command to Aaron, "Do not drink wine or strong drink, thou nor thy sons with thee, when ye go into the tabernacle of the congregation, lest ye die; it shall be a statute forever throughout your generations (Lev. 10:1-9). The inference is that Nadab and Abihu were drunk when they went in with the strange fire.

In the case of Noah, it is the only blot on his long and devoted career. It was the deep valley experience in his life. There are many instances in the Bible of a giant in the faith falling into a trap in the latter part of his life.

Noah is the first, but not the last. One thinks of David, Solomon, Gideon, Uzziah, and Josiah. The mature, later years are often the dangerous part of a person's life. But God in His grace did not abandon his honored servant. Before the Flood he had been a preacher, but here after his devastating experience, like Jacob at the end of his life, he becomes a prophet and gives an oracle of blessing and cursing concerning the future of his sons which has immense significance:

"And Noah awoke from his wine, and knew what his younger son had done unto him. And he said, Cursed be Canaan; a servant of servants shall he be unto his brethren. And he said, Blessed be the Lord God of Shem; and Canaan shall be his servant. God shall enlarge Japheth, and he shall dwell in the tents of Shem; and Canaan shall be his servant."

It is remarkable that the curse is upon Canaan, and his father Ham is not mentioned in the oracle. Three times the word "servant" is used of Canaan and to emphasize it, he is to be a "servant of servants."

There is a definite link between the oracle of chapter 9 and the table of nations in chapter 10, where the genealogy of the three sons of Noah and the consequent three branches of the human race are outlined. History has verified Noah's predictions in the oracle.

As we look down through the ages, we find the Canaanite in possession of the Promised Land at the time of the patriarchs: "And the border of the Canaanites was from Sidon, as thou comest to Gerar, unto Gaza; as thou goest unto Sodom and Gomorrah" (Gen. 10:19).

When Abraham arrived in the land of promise, "the Canaanite was then in the land" (Gen. 12:6). The mention of Sodom and Gomorrah gives an idea of the moral condition of the Canaanite. God had to destroy them with fire and brimstone. Leviticus 18 gives a list of the unnatural sexual sins practiced by the Canaanite population and from which the people of Israel were commanded to abstain. The word, "nakedness" is used twenty-four times. The wicked, debased life-style had deteriorated to such an extent that God had to order their extermination. This was only partially carried out by Joshua at the invasion of the land. The curse on Canaan was foreseen and fulfilled.

In Shem, we see the blessing of carrying the Messianic line. The first promise was that the seed of the woman would crush the serpent's head (Gen. 3:15, JND). From Shem, it comes down through Abraham and David to the Babe of Bethlehem, to the Cross, and finally to the Throne.

Japheth finds shelter in the tents of Shem. God has not forgotten the teeming millions of the Gentiles. The gospel of salvation was for the Jew first, but also for the Greek.

It is interesting that in the three detailed conversions recorded in Acts 8-10, the first is a son of Ham, the Ethiopian eunuch; the second a son of Shem, Saul of Tarsus; the third a son of Japheth, Cornelius, the Roman soldier. Under grace there is no respect of persons. The good news of salvation is for every tribe and tongue and nation.

ADDENDUM

Noah was born circa BC 2948. He died circa BC 1998, aged 950 years. He was the tenth from Adam through Seth. Born 126 years after the death of Adam, he was contemporary with Terah for 128 years, and with Abram for almost fifty years (Young's Concordance).

As an historical character, he is attested by Moses (Gen. 6-9); by Isaiah (Isa. 54:9); by Ezekiel (Ezek. 14:14, 20); by the Lord Jesus (Matt. 24:37-38); by Peter (1 Pet. 3:20; 2 Pet. 2:5); and is included in the honor roll of faith (Heb. 11:7).

Job mentions the flood (22:16) as did the Lord and Peter (Matt. 24:38-39; 2 Pet. 2:5).

2
Abraham & Mount Moriah

The Man in the Middle

Abraham is one of the key figures in human history. He appears in the Scriptures exactly halfway between Adam and Christ, approximately 2,000 years after the creation of Adam and 2,000 years before the incarnation of the Messiah. His life and testimony is an epoch in the purposes of God for mankind. Its importance is shown by the fact that the first eleven chapters of Genesis relates the history of the human race up to the call of Abram by God, and from that point, the rest of the Old Testament traces the record of his descendants, the Hebrew people. He was descended through Eber in the ninth generation (Gen. 10:21) from Shem, the eldest son of Noah in the direct Messianic line (Luke 4:34). In the New Testament, his importance is further emphasized by the space given to him in the great list of the heroes of faith recorded in Hebrews 11.

Abraham was born in Mesopotamia, the son of Terah (Gen. 11:26). His original name was Abram, meaning "height." His wife's name was Sarai. Many years later, God made a covenant with him and changed his name to Abraham, "Father of a multitude," and his wife's name to Sarah, meaning "Princess" (Gen. 17:15). He had a long life of 175 years, and on two occasions he is called "The Friend of God" (Isa. 41:8; Jas. 2:23).

THE CALL OF ABRAHAM

"The God of glory appeared unto our father Abraham, when he was in Mesopotamia before he dwelt in Charran, and said unto him, Get thee out of thy country, and from thy kindred, and come into the land which I shall show thee" (Acts 7:2-3). Apparently the call of God came to Abram when he was living in Ur of the Chaldees, a flourishing city with a highly developed civilization. It was situated in southern Mesopotamia, not far from the spot where the Euphrates empties into the Persian Gulf.

In recent times, it has been excavated by a number of archaeologists, notably by C. Leonard Woolley (1922-34). He uncovered the Royal Tombs of Ur which produced a treasure of magnificent golden vessels, musical instruments, and weapons of war that caused a sensation comparable to the discovery of King Tutankhamen's tomb in Egypt. The city was encompassed by a wall two and a half miles around and 77 feet thick. It had a complex hierarchy of government and a well-developed system of commerce. There were two-storied houses, some with ten or twelve rooms. Schools had a varied curriculum including reading, writing, and mathematics The most prominent feature of the city was a ziggurat or artificial mountain made of sundried bricks, 200x150x70 feet high. On top was a shrine dedicated to Nanna, the Moon-god, the deity of Ur. The ziggurat was called "the mountain of God." Many of the homes had a domestic shrine for worship.

Joshua 24:2 informs us: "Thus saith the Lord God of Israel, Your fathers dwelt of old on the other side of the river, even Terah, the father of Abraham, and the father of Nachor; and they served other gods." This is the background and environment in which Abram lived and was brought up. But then the God of glory appeared and said, "Get out!" It was the primary revelation of God to His servant.

The original call of God at Ur was obeyed. He left all the wealth, sophistication, and security of a settled life, but also its pagan worship, and went out as a pilgrim and a stranger, not knowing where he was going. The God of glory had told him to go and that was sufficient.

He did not go alone. His wife Sarai, his father Terah, and his nephew Lot went with him. They journeyed 600 miles northwest to Haran and there stopped. The Lord had called Abram, but apparently his father Terah took over command of the emigrating party. "Terah took Abram his son, and Lot the son of Haran his son's son, and Sarai his daughter-in-law, his son Abram's wife; and they went forth with them from Ur of the Chaldees, to go into the land of Canaan, and they came unto Haran and dwelt there. And the days of Terah were 205 years: and Terah died in Haran" (Gen. 11:31-32).

Haran was on the border between Mesopotamia and Canaan. The great river Euphrates separated the two countries. One can understand Terah's feelings. To cross the river was a complete break with the old life and land. But he died! Abram was now free to act. The hindrance to complete obedience was now removed. Many today encounter this difficulty when they attempt to obey the call of God. "A man's foes shall be they of his own household. He that loveth father or mother more than Me is not worthy of Me" (Matt. 10:36-37).

On leaving his native land and facing the unknown future, Abram received a promise from God: "I will make of thee a great nation, and I will bless thee, and make thy name great, and thou shalt be a blessing. And I will bless them that bless thee, and curse him that curseth thee; and in thee shall all families of the earth be blessed" (Gen. 12:2-3). This was the firstfruits of a covenant, later to be ratified and amplified.

ABRAM A BUILDER OF ALTARS

On arrival in the land of Canaan, Abram's first act was to

build an altar. This was the first of four altars, a place of worship and fresh revelation.

1) "And Abram passed through the land unto the place of Shechem, unto the oak of Moreh. And the Canaanite was still in the land. And the Lord appeared unto Abram and said, Unto thy seed will I give this land: and there builded he an altar unto the Lord, who appeared unto him." This altar is connected with *promise* (ch. 12:6-7).

2) "And he removed from there unto a mountain on the east of Bethel, and pitched his tent, having Bethel on the west and Hai on the east; and there he builded an altar unto the Lord, and called upon the name of the Lord." This altar is linked with *prayer* (ch. 12:8).

3) "And the Lord said unto Abram, after Lot was separated from him, Lift up now thine eyes, and look from the place where thou art northward, and southward, and eastward, and westward, for all the land which thou seest, to thee will I give it, and to thy seed forever. And I will make thy seed as the dust of the earth, so that if a man can number the dust of the earth, then shall thy seed also be numbered . . . Then Abram removed his tent and came and dwelt by the oaks of Mamre, which is in Hebron, and built there an altar unto the Lord." This altar is the response of faith to the *promise* of the land and the seed (ch. 13:14-18).

4) The fourth and final altar is on Mount Moriah. Here is the climax of Abraham's obedience, sacrifice and faith. It was rewarded by a new revelation of God's name, Jehovah-jireh. The Lord saw, the Lord *provided* (ch. 22).

THE REVELATION OF THE NAME OF GOD TO ABRAHAM

God reveals Himself in at least four ways: In creation, in His Word, in His Son, the Lord Jesus Christ, and in His Names. Abraham is the head of a new race, the dynasty of faith, and God granted him at critical points in his life a sevenfold revelation in a series of meaningful Names. They are:

1) *The God of glory* (Acts 7:2). At a difficult period in Moses' life, he prayed, "I beseech Thee, show me Thy glory" (Ex. 33:18). Isaiah and Ezekiel too had that experience (Isa. 6; Ezek. 1).

2) *Jehovah* (Gen. 12:1-8). Six times, the covenant promising and keeping God is mentioned: Abram called by Jehovah (v. 1); Jehovah appeared unto him (v. 7); he built an altar unto Jehovah (v. 7); and he called upon the name of Jehovah (v. 8).

3) *El Elyon*, The Most High God (Gen. 14:18-24). This is the first occurrence of this title of God in Scripture. Here it is used of the Melchizedek priesthood. Note its use in Deuteronomy 32:8 and in Daniel 3-5.

4) *Adonai*, Sovereign Lord or Master (Gen. 15:2). It is used concerning Abram's refusal of the riches of Sodom.

5) *El Shaddai*, God Almighty or All-sufficient (Gen. 17:1). This is used concerning patient waiting for the promised heir.

6) *El Olam*, The Everlasting God (Gen. 21:33). The God of the Ages was called to witness Abraham's covenant.

7) *Jehovah-jireh*, The Lord saw, the Lord provided (Gen. 22:14).

The revelation of these seven names to Abraham mark seven steps in his life of faith from his call to leave Ur of the Chaldees, to his supreme test on Mount Moriah.

ABRAHAM: THE MAN OF FAITH

Abraham has been called the father of the faithful (Rom. 4:1). He occupies an important position in that great chapter of the heroes of faith, Hebrews 11, and rightly so. The records describe not only seven steps in his life of faith, but also seven tests of his faith. After his call to leave Ur, the first test was:

Family: Arriving at Haran, his father Terah refused to cross the river Euphrates which separated his homeland from Canaan. We do not know how long he was delayed, but when Terah died, he obeyed the original command and crossed the river. From that time on, he was known as the

33

"Hebrew" (the man from across the river). He never retraced his steps to go back to Ur. His next test was:

Famine (12:10): The famines recorded in Scripture are full of spiritual lessons. Hunger can be a severe trial. Hearing of plenty in Egypt, the pilgrim band headed for that land which resulted in a third test, that of:

Fear: He was afraid that his life would be in danger on account of his beautiful wife, Sarai. Calling her his sister, Abram found that his fears were justified, when Pharoah sent for Sarai, and took her into his home. But God was good to his erring servant, by warning Pharoah not to touch the woman. Abram got out of Egypt, a humiliated but wiser man. A fourth test was:

Friction: Both he and his nephew Lot were wealthy. Problems arose among the herdsmen of their respective flocks, and it became necessary to separate. Abram graciously gave the younger man the choice of location. Lot, influenced by what he saw in Egypt, chose the well-watered plains near Sodom, which ended in his downfall. Abram overcame that test by remaining a pilgrim with his tent and altar. A fifth test was his attitude to:

Filthy Lucre: He refused to touch the spoils of war from the soiled hands of the king of Sodom. A man's attitude to money is an acid test of his character. He had every right to the loot as he was the victor in the battle over the united kings of the East. He ignored the temptation to enrich himself from worldlings. The sixth test was:

Frustration: God had promised him an heir and posterity as numerous as the dust of the earth and as the stars of heaven. The first promise was made when Abram was 75 years old (Gen. 12:4, 7). The heir of promise was born when he was 100 years old (21:5). After ten years of waiting without result, he took matters into his own hands and married Hagar, the Egyptian handmaid. He was 86 years old when Ishmael was born. This lapse of Abram's faith in God's promise has had

34

agelong and worldwide consequences. In three of these tests of faith there was failure, and in three there was victory. But in the *Final* test, when God called upon him to offer up Isaac, there was complete triumph.

MOUNT MORIAH

The sacrifice was to be made in "the land of Moriah" (Gen. 22:2). The word "Moriah" is found only here and in 2 Chronicles 3:1. The name means "Jah provides" (Young). It is associated with Abraham and Isaac (Gen. 22), Araunah's threshing floor (2 Sam. 24:18-25), and with Solomon's temple (2 Chron. 3). It is said that Golgotha, on which the crucifixion of the Saviour took place, was a spur of the mountain on which Solomon's temple was built. In ancient times, a road was cut that separates the temple mount from the Golgotha spur. It was God who selected the mountain spot where Abraham was to offer his son Isaac, the temple was to be built, and where His Beloved Son was to suffer for the sin of the world. A sacred spot indeed!

The Command: "Take now thy son, thine only son Isaac, whom thou lovest, and get thee into the land of Moriah; and offer him there for a burnt offering upon one of the mountains that I will tell thee of" (v. 2).

There are five important expressions in this chapter that occur for the first time in Scripture. As the keys to the passage, they are:

1) Thine only son. This is found three times (vv. 2, 12, 16). In the N.T., John uses the Greek equivalent (*monogenes*) five times of the Lord Jesus, the Only Begotten (John 1:14, 18; 3:16, 18; 1 John 4:9)—the Unique One (cf. Rom. 8:3, 32).

2) Love (v. 2). This first occurrence refers to the love of a father for his son (cf. John 5:20; 10:17; 17:26). The second occurrence of the word (Gen. 24:67), unfolds the love of a bridegroom for his bride.

3) Worship (v. 5). Translated "bowed" down (Gen. 18:2;

35

19:1, A.V.), it involves giving the best to God (cf. Matt. 2:2, 11).

4) Lamb (vv. 7, 8). Where is the Lamb? The New Testament answer is found in John 1:29.

5) Obeyed (v. 18). This was the immediate response to the command of the Lord.

The Communion: They "went both of them together" (v. 8; cf. v. 19). It was three days' journey from Beer-sheba, "the well of the oath" to the place of sacrifice. This reminds us of the three years' communion and fellowship between the Father and the Son from the river Jordan to Calvary. The Gospel writers take up this theme: "And in the morning, rising up a great while before day, He went out, and departed into a solitary place, and there prayed" (Mark 1:35). The apostle John, especially, describes the Father and Son relationship. In his Gospel, he mentions the Father 120 times and the Son about 45 times.

There may have been periods of silence between Abraham and Isaac on that long journey; they are not recorded. But it is evident that they were of one mind in carrying out God's command—Abraham in his determination, and Isaac in his subjection and obedience. On the third day, Abraham lifted up his eyes and saw the place afar off. This was the time and the place when the servants and the ass were left behind, the spot where Abraham's faith grasped the great truth of death and resurrection. The last sentence of verse 5 makes this plain: "I and the lad will go yonder and worship, and come again to you." The sacrifice of Isaac he regarded as "worship," and Isaac as well as his father was to "come again." This is all the more remarkable seeing he carried both a knife and the fire, the instruments of death. The wood was laid on Isaac. The fire would consume the burnt offering. In all of Abraham's experience he had never seen or heard of a resurrection from the dead.

The Conversation (vv. 7-8): Finally the silence between the father and the son is broken by Isaac's question and Abraham's answer. "And Isaac spake unto Abraham his father, and said, My father; and he said, Here am I, my son. And he said, Behold the fire and the wood; but where is the lamb for a burnt offering? And Abraham said, My son, God will provide Himself a lamb for a burnt offering; so they went both of them together."

There is not another word from Isaac, but what a wealth of meaning lies behind both the question and the answer! Some commentators suggest that Abraham spoke evasively, but rather it was the long sight of faith. Hebrews 11:17-19 declares, "By faith Abraham, when he was tried, offered up Isaac; and he that had received the promises offered up his only begotten son, of whom it was said, That in Isaac shall thy seed be called; accounting that God was able to raise him up, even from the dead; from whence also he received him in a figure." The force of the word "accounting" means that he argued the situation in his own mind, and on the basis of God's promises came to a definite conclusion. It is the highest peak of Abraham's faith. From the standpoint of volition, surrender and obedience, Isaac was really offered. But God in a wonderful way provided a substitute. The answer to Isaac's question, "Where is the lamb?" is given in John 1:29, "Behold the Lamb of God, which taketh away the sin of the world."

The Crisis (vv. 7-8): "And they came to the place which God had told him of" (v. 9). The place is mentioned four times (vv. 3, 4, 9, 14). It was a place chosen by God—Mount Moriah—the place where God had placed His Name (Deut. 12:13-14), the place where the temple was built, the place of gathering and sacrifice. In connection with the fulfillment of that which was anticipated in Genesis, the Gospels mention the word "place" four times:

A place called Gethsemane (Mk. 14:32).

A place called Gabbatha (John 19:13).

A place called Golgotha (John 19:17).

"Come, see the place (the Garden Tomb) where the Lord lay" (Matt. 28:6). This must have been the most sacred place on earth! Judas knew the place (John 18:2) where the Lord had agonized in view of the cross, but sadly and tragically, he went to his own place (Acts 1:25).

And "Abraham built an altar there, and laid the wood in order, and bound Isaac his son, and laid him on the altar upon the wood." This is Abraham's fourth altar. The other three, at Shechem, Bethel/Hai, and Hebron, led up to it and prepared him for it. The altar on Mount Moriah was the final test and the climax of his faith. Between verses 9 and 13, the conjunction "and" occurs ten times. It is not eloquent grammatically, but it shows either the continuity and persistence, or word of remonstrance on his part. His experience must have typified that which our Lord passed through in a supremely greater measure in Gethsemane and on the cross.

Verses 10 to 12 graphically relate the extent to which Abraham's faith was tested. His uplifted hand holding the knife was about to strike. At the last possible moment, the Angel of the Lord intervened. His obedience had been tested to the full, and had stood the test. He had not withheld his only son. This proved beyond doubt that he believed in the God of resurrection. It also points forward to an infinitely greater sacrifice when God "spared not his own Son, but delivered Him up for us all" (Rom. 8:32). The voice from heaven arrested the deathblow on Isaac, but at Golgotha, amid the darkness, heaven was silent.

After the voice, Abraham's eyes were immediately directed to a God-provided substitute for a sacrifice on the altar. Looking behind him he saw, not a lamb, but a ram, caught in a thicket by its horns. Later, in the Levitical economy, the ram, the leader of the flock, was used in the trespass offering (Lev. 5:15), and in the consecration of the priest for a burnt offering (8:18). Here it is, a burnt offering "in the stead of" his son. Although the word "substitute" does not occur in the text, here we see in the sacrificial death of the ram that which the word means. Thus we have in this incident another glorious type of the substitutionary death of the Saviour on the cross. Abraham recognized the wonderful way in which God had provided the substitute for a burnt offering by naming the place Jehovah-jireh, "the Lord will provide."

THE ABRAHAMIC COVENANT

In verses 15 to 18, the Abrahamic covenant was confirmed and expanded. The Angel of the Lord spoke twice from heaven, firstly averting the deathblow upon Isaac and assuring Abraham of the completeness of his obedience (v. 12). The second time (vv. 15-18), he pronounces a fourfold blessing on the patriarch and his seed: "By Myself have I sworn, saith the Lord, for because thou hast done this thing, and hast not withheld thy son, thine only son; that in blessing I will bless thee, and in multiplying, I will multiply thy seed as the stars of heaven, and as the sand which is upon the seashore; and thy seed shall possess the gate of his enemies; and in thy seed shall all the nations of the earth be blessed; because thou hast obeyed My voice."

This is the occasion referred to in Hebrews 6:13-20, when God confirmed the promise of a seed to Abraham and sealed it with an oath. First the seed is compared to the dust of the earth, then to the stars of heaven, and now to the sand of the seashore; an earthly seed, a heavenly seed, and then a seed that would reach out to the nations. Galatians 3:16 tells us that that Seed (in the singular) is Christ in whom all the nations of the earth will be blessed. All this blessing is guaranteed by the promise and the mighty oath of God. In this we can rest. It must not be forgotten that the Abrahamic Covenant also involves the promise of a land with clearly defined boundaries (Gen. 15:18-21). The promises concerning both the seed and the land will be fully implemented and fulfilled in a coming day.

39

This great chapter, Genesis 22, is closed by a genealogy, introducing Rebekah who is destined to be the bride of Isaac (Gen. 24). What a fitting conclusion to the narrative of Isaac, who, in his miraculous birth, his submission to the will of his father, in his figurative death and resurrection, and then in his marriage to Rebekah, is a type of the Lord Jesus.

As we look back over the intensely interesting narrative of Abraham, "the friend of God," we can see that he had deep valley experiences in his life—when he went down into Egypt and denied his wife; and doubted God's promise of an heir when he married the Egyptian slave girl with all its devastating results. But his faith in the "God of glory" made him a pilgrim and a stranger, resulted in justification by faith, and finally led him to the mountaintop of Moriah where his obedience, dedication, and faith in the God of resurrection was fully demonstrated. He looked for a city which hath foundations, whose builder and maker is God. What an inspiration he is to those who are in the valley of doubt or depression today, but whose faith rests on the same eternal foundations laid on the Person and the substitutionary death of our heavenly Isaac, the only begotten Son of God.

3
Moses & Mount Sinai

The Emancipator

In the course of human history, Moses was one of the greatest men who ever lived. Few men ever influenced mankind as he did. He towers above not only his contemporaries, but succeeding generations as well. In the Bible, his name occurs 835 times in the Old Testament and 80 times in the New Testament, more frequently than any other O. T. character. He wrote 137 chapters of the Bible, is the author of the Pentateuch and his name occurs as the writer of Psalm 90, where he is called "the Man of God." He is designated a prophet (Deut. 18:15); a priest (Ps. 99:6); and a king in Jeshurun (Deut. 33:5). If Abraham is the father of his people and his country, demonstrating the principle of faith, Moses is the emancipator of his people from slavery, symbolizing the principle of leadership.

It would be interesting to ask wherein lay the secret of his greatness and his power? First of all, it lay in God's sovereignty in choosing and raising up a man at a critical point in world history; and secondly, that man's willingness to subject himself to God's will and obey His commands. He was the instrument in God's hands to carry out His purposes of grace for His people.

Moses' life of 120 years is divided into three equal periods of forty years. The first forty years was spent in Egypt. Born of God-fearing parents, living as slaves under an oppressive, tyrannical government, by a series of remarkable divinely overruled events, the baby Moses was adopted by the daughter of the reigning Pharoah. His Jewish mother was hired to care for him. As a protegé of the royal household, he was given the best education that the most advanced nation in the world at that time had to offer. Stephen, in Acts 7:22, tells us that "Moses was learned in all the wisdom of the Egyptians, and was mighty in words and in deeds." God was molding and preparing him for his life's work and allowing the devil to pay for it.

MOSES' CHOICE

"By faith Moses, when he was come to years, refused to be called the son of Pharoah's daughter; choosing rather to suffer affliction with the people of God, than to enjoy the pleasures of sin for a season; esteeming the reproach of Christ greater riches than the treasures of Egypt; for he had respect unto the recompense of the reward" (Heb. 11:24-26). It was the turning point in his life. He turned his back upon wealth, affluence, false religion, and all that the world had to offer, and identified himself with a suffering nation of slaves. But they were his own kin. Seeing an Egyptian overseer maltreating a Hebrew, he lost his self-control, impetuously slew the Egyptian and hid his body in the sand. He had acted hastily and as a result had to flee from the country.

The next forty years were spent in obscurity on the backside of the desert in the land of Midian. Instead of the schools of Egypt and its opulent life-style, he was introduced to the discipline of God's school. Instead of a royal protegé, he became a father and a shepherd of sheep. The lessons learned in the home and in the humble occupation of taking care of the sheep fitted him for that which lay ahead in leading a nation.

42

No one is fitted to counsel on the problems of family life until they have been in the school of suffering with God. Practical experience is a hard but valuable teacher. An act of anger performed in a moment of time took Moses out of Egypt, but it took forty hard years in a lonely desert to take Egyptian mentality out of him. This is a school where many of God's honored servants have been trained: eg., Elijah, John the Baptist, and Paul.The first part of Moses' training in Egypt was valuable, but the second in the desert was indispensable.

MOSES' CALL AND COMMISSION

While tending the flock, Moses saw a bush burning with fire, and yet it was not consumed. The time had come for his call to his life's work. The burning bush was the first of a series of sign miracles in which God dealt with four parts of his body:

1) *His Feet:* As Moses approached the burning bush to see the amazing sight, God spoke: "Moses, Moses . . . Put off thy shoes from off thy feet, for the place whereon thou standest is holy ground." His first lesson was reverence in the presence of God. This was to be a primary trait in Moses' life. In our modern life, reverence for God is rapidly deteriorating. In addressing God in prayer and worship, and speaking about Him in ministry and evangelism, we would appeal for reverence. The familiar language of the street or the telling of jokes to provoke a laugh, should find no place in the ministry of the man who has been in the presence of the Almighty Sovereign of the Universe.

2) *His Hand:* "And the Lord said unto him, What is that in thy hand? And he said, A rod. And He said, Cast it on the ground. And he cast it on the ground, and it became a serpent; and Moses fled from before it. And the Lord said unto Moses, Put forth thy hand and take it by the tail. And he put forth his hand and caught it, and it became a rod in his hand." The lesson is obvious. The rod was the shepherd's rod

with which he tended the sheep. Later in Scripture it was to become the scepter, and a rod of iron (Ps. 2:9; Rev. 2:27). It is the symbol of authority and rule. In man's hand it symbolizes delegated authority. Moses was to use it five times in his subsequent life. The first man to have the rod of dominion or authority was Adam (Gen. 1:26, 28). In his case it was cast to the ground and became a deadly serpent. But another Man, the Last Adam, has crushed the serpent's head. Moses, the servant, boldly took it by the tail and it again became a rod in his hand. With it he faced Pharoah, opened the Red Sea, smote the rock to bring out the living water, and confronted Amalek, the enemy of the people (Ex. 17:9). Our Lord, in the Great Commission, said: "All authority in heaven and in earth has been committed unto Me; go ye therefore . . . " Blessed is the man who has "the ordination of the pierced hands" and who carries the rod of delegated authority from the risen and glorified Christ in his hand.

3) *His Bosom:* "And the Lord said furthermore unto him, Put now thy hand into thy bosom. And he put his hand into his bosom; and when he took it out, behold his hand was leprous as snow. And he said again, Put thy hand into thy bosom again; and plucked it out of his bosom, and behold, it was turned again as his other flesh." Here is the lesson of the seat of human depravity and corruption. Paul said: "In me, that is in my flesh dwelleth no good thing." The servant that goes forth into the work of the Lord and who has never learned this lesson, is of all men to be pitied. The old man and the flesh, the old habits and desires, and the depraved sinful nature are still with us. We are exhorted to put off the old man with his deeds, and to crucify or put to death the flesh (Rom. 6:6-23). But they are with us as long as life shall last and there is plenty of tinder in our bosom on which Satan can cast his fiery darts and set it alight. But thank God for the indwelling Spirit of life in Christ Jesus, and the Word of God, and the Intercessor at God's right hand to give us the victory

in time of need. The world outside, the flesh inside, and the devil beneath us have not changed. But we can be overcomers through Christ Jesus our Lord.

4) *His mouth:* "And Moses said unto the Lord, O my Lord, I am not eloquent, neither heretofore, nor since Thou hast spoken unto Thy servant, but I am slow of speech, and of a slow tongue. And the Lord said unto him, Who hath made man's mouth? Have not I the Lord?"

Moses' words were just an excuse. He did not want to go back to Egypt and face Pharoah. In Egypt he was too hasty; now he is too hesitant. Most preachers at the beginning of their career feel the same way. Very few are eloquent or facile speakers. Usually it means hard work and careful study and only develops through time and experience. Mere volubility and talkativeness is a frightening talent. An endless talker who must have the floor at all times is a terrible bore and affliction. But what a comfort it is when God says: "Now therefore go, and I will be with thy mouth, and teach thee what thou shalt say!" And what a joy it is when one feels that the Holy Spirit is speaking, unquenched and ungrieved, and God's people are being blessed and refreshed by the spoken word. The Apostle James has a lot to say about the tongue, both good and bad. So conscious did Moses become of his own insufficiency, that God had practically to thrust him out into the work for which He had called and fitted him. It reminds us of the words:

> "How ready is that man to go,
> Whom God has never sent;
> How timorous, diffident, and slow
> God's chosen instrument."

THE REVELATION OF GOD'S NAME

After his call and commission at the burning bush, Moses was anxious to know the name of the One who had called

45

and sent him, first to the Israelites and then to Pharoah in Egypt. Note, first of all, the location. It was "the mountain of God, Horeb" (Ex. 3:1) This is the first of seventeen mentions of Horeb in the Bible. It is the northeastern peak of the mountain range of which Mount Sinai is the northwestern.

The One who appeared and spoke to him out of the burning bush is called "The Angel of the Lord" (v. 2). He is called "Jehovah" (v. 4). Then He speaks in verse 6, "I am the God of thy father, the God of Abraham, the God of Isaac, and the God of Jacob. And Moses hid his face; for he was afraid to look upon God."

"And Moses said unto God, Behold, when I come unto the children of Israel, and shall say unto them, The God of your fathers hath sent me unto you; and they shall say unto me, What is His name? what shall I say unto them? And God said unto Moses, I AM THAT I AM; and he said, Thus shalt thou say unto the children of Israel, I AM hath sent me unto you. And God said moreover unto Moses, thus shalt thou say unto the children of Israel, The Lord God of your fathers, the God of Abraham, the God of Isaac, and the God of Jacob, hath sent me unto you; this is My name forever, and this is My memorial to all generations" (vv. 13-15).

This is one of the greatest revelations in Holy Scripture of the names of God. I AM THAT I AM is an exposition of the mystic name Yahweh or Jehovah or LORD. It contains each tense of the verb "to be." It could be translated, I was always being, I am always being, I shall always continue to be. Here it is the present continuous tense—I AM. It is His name as the self-existent One, an expression of the essential being of God. It was this name that the Lord Jesus claimed when He said to the unbelieving Jews, "Before Abraham was, I AM" (John 8:58). In His ministry He used it at least seven times: I AM the Bread of Life. I AM the good Shepherd. I AM the Door. I AM the Way, the Truth and the Life. I AM the Light of the world. I AM the Resurrection and the Life. I AM the true Vine. In Gethsemane, when the soldiers from the chief priests came to arrest Him, He asked them, Whom seek ye? They answered, Jesus, of Nazareth, He replied, I AM. As soon as He said this, they went backward and fell to the ground. The synoptic Gospels describe the Lord Jesus in Gethsemane falling on the ground in prayer, in His agony and blood-like sweat, but John sees Him on His feet in royal majesty and dignity uttering the divine title I AM twice and His enemies on the ground before Him. John, in his introduction to the book of Revelation, uses the majestic, divine title twice: "Grace be unto you, and peace, from Him who is, and who was, and who is to come, and from the seven spirits who are before His throne" (Rev. 1:4); "I am Alpha and Omega, the beginning and the ending, saith the Lord, who is, and who was, and who is to come, the Almighty" (v. 8). "The same, yesterday, and today, and forever" (Heb. 13:8).

Moses, now fortified with his credentials, his call, and his commission, and with faith in the ineffable Name of Jehovah, the I AM THAT I AM, is now ready to present himself to his brethren, the children of Israel, and to their formidable oppressor, Pharoah. No man on earth was better equipped for the task. At eighty years of age, he was ready for the contest and his lifework as the emancipator of his people.

THE PASSOVER AND THE EXODUS

Moses was an expert, both in the language and diplomacy of Egypt. During a series of interviews with Pharoah, Moses made the request, "Let My people go," reinforced by miraculous signs indicating God's power and the authority of His servant. Then followed nine different plagues, each one more severe than the last one, sent by God on the land of Egypt. Each time when Pharoah pled for mercy and the plague was removed, he reluctantly made a number of excuses and minor concessions. Five times we are told that he hardened his heart. It was evident that he had no intention of releasing

47

the people of Israel from their bondage. Then God, seeing there was no change, judicially hardened his heart. The final judgment was on the firstborn of every family in Egypt. God instructed Moses that each household of the people of Israel was to take a specially chosen lamb, in the evening of the fourteenth day of the month Nisan. It was to be sacrificed and its blood sprinkled on the two sideposts and the upper lintel of the door of their dwellings. They were to remain inside and feast on the roast lamb. The Angel of the Lord passed through the land that night, and in every house not protected by the blood of the lamb, the firstborn child was slain. This is the night of the Passover, which marks the birth of the nation of Israel. It was an epoch in human history. It points forward to another and greater epoch, when the Lamb of God was sacrificed on Calvary's cross. His precious blood is the price of our redemption from sin and slavery.

The children of Israel left Egypt in a hurry. Pharoah begged them to get out, but later changed his mind and decided to follow and destroy them. They were a mighty host— "about six hundred thousand on foot that were men, beside children. And a mixed multitude went up also with them; and flocks, and herds, even very much cattle" (Ex.12:37-38). The mixed multitude was to give trouble later on. But God was merciful in protecting them.

"And the Lord went before them by day in a pillar of cloud, to lead them in the way; and by night in a pillar of fire to give them light; to go by day and night" (13:21). Their first great problem was the crossing of the Red Sea. Shut in by the great fortress 'Migdol' which was on the 'Shur' or wall (built to protect Egypt from Asia) and the sea, with Pharoah's hosts behind, and shut in on the other side by the wilderness (Ex. 14:2-3), it was indeed a crisis. To the tacticians of Egypt, it was a perfect trap. Then the Lord ordered Moses to go forward and lift up his rod and divide the sea. The Angel of God that was in front, leading them with the pillar cloud, moved to their rear, protecting them from the enemy. The Lord caused the sea to go back by a strong east wind all that night, and made the sea dry land, and the waters were divided. The people passed over on dry land, but when the Egyptian forces attempted to follow them, the sea returned to its bed and overwhelmed them. This was celebrated by the first song in the Bible: "I will sing unto the Lord, for He hath triumphed gloriously; the horse and his rider hath He thrown into the sea" (Ex. 15:1ff.). Interestingly, the name of Moses is associated with the first song in the Bible and also with the last (Rev. 15:3).

There follow the experiences at Marah and Elim and the water (ch. 15); in the wilderness of Sin and the manna (ch. 16); and Rephidim and water from the rock, followed by the conflict with Amalek (ch. 17). Finally Moses and the people arrived at the mount of God (Ex. 3:1, 12). It was here where God had first spoken to Moses. Here he was reunited with his wife, Zipporah, and his two sons, Gershom and Eliezer, and his father-in-law, Jethro, the priest of Midian. Jethro gave him some good advice about sharing responsibility with able men, who fear God—men of truth who hate covetousness. This sane counsel would be a help in the difficult days that lay ahead.

MOSES AND MOUNT SINAI

The Peninsula of the Sinai is triangular, shaped like a heart, situated between two arms of the Red Sea. On the west is the Gulf of Suez, and on the east is the Gulf of Aqaba (or the Gulf of Eilat). The west shore is 180 miles long, the east shore about 130, the north borderline about 150. The northern part is relatively flat desert, but in the south is a great cluster of rugged mountains. Two biblical names are associated with these, Horeb being the whole mountain group, and Sinai, a special mountain in the range. Its modern name is Jebel Musa (the Mountain of Moses). It is an isolated mass of rock, rising abruptly from the plain in awesome grandeur. On the north-west side is a spacious plain, two miles long and half a mile wide, capable of accommodating two million people. Moses must have been very familiar with the area. He had spent fortyyears in the desert around, taking care of sheep, and it was at Horeb that God had first spoken and revealed Himself to him (Ex. 3:1-6). Now he has to lead and care for another larger flock, the people of Israel.

The journey of Israel from Egypt to Sinai terminated on the third month. There they camped before the mount (Ex. 19:1-2). They remained there one whole year (Num. 1:1). Here God was to reveal Himself through Moses to the people. Apparently Moses ascended the mount four times, twice for an undefined duration of time and twice for a period of forty days. Each time there was a distinct revelation. They are as follows:

1) *God proposes a conditional covenant with Israel* (Ex. 19:3-19). He reminds them of their redemption from the bondage of Egypt and how he bore them on eagles' wings and brought them to Himself. "Now therefore if ye will obey My voice indeed and keep My covenant, then ye shall be a peculiar treasure unto Me above all people, for all the earth is Mine. And ye shall be unto Me a kingdom of priests and an holy nation." When Moses conveyed the terms of the covenant to the people, they replied: "All that the Lord hath spoken we will do." Alas, they did not realize their own weakness and consequent failure as subsequent history records. All the previous covenants that God made were with individuals, with Noah, Abraham, Isaac, and Jacob, but here for the first time it is with a nation.

2) *The second ascent of the mount by Moses* (Ex. 19:20). It was accompanied by a tremendous display of God's majesty and glory. The people were told to wash and sanctify themselves, and not to come near or touch the mountain. "And Mount Sinai was altogether on a smoke, because the Lord descended upon it in fire, and the smoke thereof ascended as the smoke

of a furnace, and the whole mount quaked greatly. And when the voice of the trumpet sounded long, and (became) louder and louder, Moses spoke, and God answered him by a voice." It was here that Moses received the Law and communicated it to the people. It was in three parts:

a) The Ten Commandments (ch. 20)—the moral law.

b) The Judgments (ch. 21-23)—the civil law.

c) The Ordinances (ch. 24-31)—laws concerning worship, the Feasts and the Sabbath. These were first communicated orally.

3) *The first forty days* (ch. 24-31). This was introduced by the ratification of the covenant by a blood sacrifice. Moses, Aaron, Nadab, Abihu, and seventy of the elders of Israel took part in the ceremony. An altar was built, with twelve pillars representing the twelve tribes. The terms and details of the covenant were written by Moses in a book. Half of the blood of the sacrifice of the burnt and peace offerings was sprinkled on the altar, and after reading to the people the terms of the covenant, they replied "All that the Lord hath said we will do and be obedient." Then the rest of the blood was sprinkled on the book and on the people (Heb. 9:19).

After a preliminary vision of God—seen by Moses, Aaron, Nadab, Abihu, and the seventy elders of Israel where they ate and drank a sacred meal—Moses alone went up into the mount and was there forty days and forty nights (Ex. 24:18).

It was during this time that he saw a model and received instructions concerning the building of the Tabernacle, the priesthood and the offerings, and the two tables of stone with the law inscribed by the finger of God (Ex. 25-31). This very important section of the Word of God has typical lessons for us at the present day. The law was inexorable in its demands for obedience, but God in His grace provided the tabernacle, the priesthood, and a system of sacrifices as a way of access to Himself. They are authorized types. The tabernacle, for example, is a pattern of things in the heavens (Heb. 8:5; 9:9, 23, 24).

The details are not left to our imagination. It is heaven transferred to earth as a visible type (Cf. references to heaven in Rev. 4, etc.) The tabernacle is a picture of:

a) The church as the house of God (Heb. 3:1-6).

b) The Person and Work of Christ (Heb. 8:2; 9:11).

c) The way of access to God (Heb. 10:20).

d) The priesthood and offerings are typical of the High Priestly ministry of Christ and His atoning sacrifice on the cross. The Epistle to the Hebrews and the Book of Revelation are divine commentaries on these great types.

THE APOSTASY AND ITS AFTERMATH (EX. 32)

When Moses came down from the mount with the tables of stone in his hand, he saw a deplorable sight and, unfortunately, his own brother Aaron was the leading figure in it. The people who so recently had pledged their allegiance to a covenant with Jehovah and had vowed to obey Him, are now worshipping a golden calf manufactured by Aaron and saying, "These are our gods which brought us up out of Egypt." They must have thought that Moses had died amid the smoke and fire of Sinai, and couldn't wait for six weeks for his return. Such is human nature and fickleness. After their worship of the golden calf, the people sat down to eat and drink and rose up to play. Moses must have been heartbroken. When God threatened to act in judgment and wipe them out, Moses interceded for them but proceeded to take drastic action. He smashed the tables of stone at the foot of the mount. Then he burned the golden calf and ground it to powder, mixed it with water, and forced the people to drink it. Then he pitched a tent outside the camp and called on all those who wished to follow the Lord to join him. All the sons of Levi did so. He ordered each man to take a sword and go throughout the camp and slay every man his fellow. That day about three thousand men were executed.

We can understand Moses' reaction to these events: Is it

worth going on? His resource was to call upon God. He made two requests: "Show me now Thy way that I may know Thee." The divine answer was: "My presence shall go with thee, and I will give thee rest." Moses added: "If Thy presence go not with me, carry us not up from here."

His second request was: "I beseech Thee, show me Thy glory." The answer was one of the most wonderful manifestations of God to mortal man. "And He said, Thou canst not see My face; for there shall no man see Me, and live. And the Lord said, Behold there is a place by Me, and thou shalt stand upon a rock; and it shall come to pass, while My glory passeth by, that I will put thee in a cleft of the rock, and will cover thee with My hand while I pass by; and I will take away My hand, and thou shalt see My back (or after-glow); but My face shall not be seen." Fortified by these two great experiences, Moses was prepared to resume his work.

THE SECOND FORTY DAYS ON THE MOUNT

With the two fresh tables of stone in his hand which he had hewed at the command of the Lord, Moses ascended Mount Sinai (Ex. 34:1-4). Again he met the Lord who proclaimed His Name and attributes, and Moses bowed his head to the earth and worshipped. The Lord renewed His covenant with Israel and recommissioned Moses, and repeated the promises concerning the occupation of the Promised Land. The feasts and the sabbaths were to be carefully observed as well as the civil and ceremonial codes of the law. He was commanded to write these words, "For after the tenor of these words I have made a covenant with thee and with Israel. And he was there with the Lord forty days and forty nights; he did neither eat bread nor drink water. And he wrote upon the tables the words of the covenant, the Ten Commandments" (vv. 27-28).

One result of this period of communion with God on the mountaintop was that the skin of his face shone, although he himself did not know it. Aaron and the people were afraid to come near him, so he put a veil on his face when speaking with them. When speaking to God, however, he took the veil off. At the burning bush, God dealt with his feet, his hand and his bosom, teaching him important lessons (Ex. 3-4). But here it is the transformation of his countenance as a result of being in the presence of God. Paul refers to this in 2 Corinthians 3:6-18. He points out the difference between the ministry of the law which results in condemnation, and the superior ministry of the new covenant: "But we all, with unveiled face reflecting as a mirror the glory of the Lord, are transformed into the same image from glory to glory, even as from the Lord the Spirit" (v. 18, R. V.)

The final chapters of Exodus (35-40) relate the historical construction of the tabernacle under the supervision of Moses and the competent workmanship of Bezalel and Aholiab, two men called and fitted by God. When it was completed, God showed His approval and His presence by the Shekinah cloud and glory filling the tabernacle.

THE BELIEVER'S RELATIONSHIP TO THE LAW OF MOSES TODAY

This is expounded in detail in Paul's Epistles to the Romans and Galatians, and in the Epistle to the Hebrews. John says, "The law was given by Moses but grace and truth came by Jesus Christ" (John 1:17). That means that there was a change of dispensation from law to grace. Paul says, "The law is holy, and the commandment holy, and just, and good" (Rom. 7:12). Why then a change? To summarize:

1) *The Law is a Standard.* Sinful man will never measure up.

2) *The Law is a Judge.* All are guilty (Rom. 1-3).

3) *The Law is an Executioner.* Its curse means death (Rom. 6:23).

4) *The Law is a Schoolmaster* (*pedegogus*) until Christ (Gal. 3:24).

Christ, the holy sinless One, fulfilled the law, bore the

curse, died a vicarious, substitutionary death on the cross. Those who believe, trust, commit themselves to Him in simple faith, in true repentance of their sin, receive eternal life and are delivered from the curse of the law.

> *Free from the law, O happy condition,*
> *Jesus hath died and there is remission.*
> *Cursed by the law, ruined by the Fall,*
> *Christ hath redeemed us once for all.* —P. P. Bliss

On the other hand, we must remember that nine of the clauses of the moral code contained in the Ten Commandments are repeated in the New Testament as incumbent on believers today. The only exception is the Sabbath. God's moral commandments and requirements do not change. But they are obeyed from a different basis and motive, that of love to Christ. James calls it the "perfect law of liberty" (Jas. 1:25). Paul describes it as "being not without law to God, but in-lawed (*lit.*) to Christ" (1 Cor. 9:21; Rom. 8:4).

MOSES IN THE WILDERNESS

The third section of Moses' life was the forty years spent in the wilderness on the way to the land of Caanan. It is the main theme of the Book of Numbers. It has been called "the record of a lost generation."At the beginning of the book, there is a census of the people in the wilderness of Sinai, and thirty-eight years later there was another in the plains of Moab, just before entering the land. Out of the two-and-a-half million who had left Egypt, the only survivors were Joshua and Caleb, the men of courage and faith. The rest left their bones in the wilderness.

The desert is the place of testing and also of God's gracious protection and provision. In Israel's case, there was dismal failure. The crucial point took place at Kadesh-barnea. Twelve men, one from each tribe, were sent ahead as spies to Canaan to survey the land and to assess their ability to occupy it. Ten came back with a pessimistic report. The enemies were too great and powerful; it would be impossible to overcome them. God had promised to be with them; their sin was unbelief in that promise. Only Joshua and Caleb said, "We are able." The result: the unbelievers were sentenced to thirty-eight years of wandering in the desert until they were wiped out. The two optimistic believers in God and His promise survived to triumphantly enter the land.

The record of the years of wandering is punctuated by a series of episodes, mostly characterized by murmuring, complaining, and revolt against the leadership of Moses. One was spearheaded by the mixed multitude that came out of Egypt with the children of Israel. It had to do with food supplies. They complained of the heavenly manna which God had miraculously provided. They longed for the variegated diet which they had enjoyed in Egypt. In response, God gave them meat in the form of flocks of quails, but it also brought judgment on the complainers.

Then there was family trouble among the leaders. Miriam and Aaron, Moses' sister and brother, spoke against him because he had married a Cushite woman. Here we are told in a parenthesis that Moses was very meek, above all the men that were upon the earth. He made no attempt to defend himself, but God intervened. Miriam was smitten with leprosy, the first time this disease is mentioned in the Bible. After seven days' exclusion from the camp, through the intercessory prayer of Moses she was healed (Num. 12).

Perhaps one of the most serious events in the history of the wilderness journey was the revolt of Korah, Dathan, and Abiram against the God-appointed leadership of Moses and Aaron (Num. 16-17). It was motivated by jealousy.

It was an attempted revolution that could have divided the people and led to disaster. It was an invasion of Levitical service into the priestly office. Again God intervened. The rebels were standing at the doors of their tents with bronze censers containing fire and incense in their hands, when suddenly the ground opened and swallowed them, and they went down alive into sheol. The disaster was accompanied by a fire from the Lord which consumed the men who had offered incense. At a subsequent undercurrent of murmuring against Moses and Aaron, who were blamed for the death of the rebels, a plague broke out in which fourteen thousand, seven hundred died.

Numbers 20 records the arrival of the whole congregation at Kadesh of notorious memory (Num. 11-14). Thirty-seven troubled years have passed since they were there. Much has happened in the meantime. The chapter opens with the death and burial of Miriam. It ends with the stripping of Aaron's garments and the putting them upon Eleazar his son, and his death and burial on the top of Mount Hor. In between is the sad story of the smiting of the rock by Moses, for which he was to die, being buried in the land of Moab.

Again the people were murmuring and complaining about the lack of water and talking about the figs and vines and pomegranates of Egypt. Again Moses and Aaron were on their faces before God. "And the Lord spake unto Moses, saying: Take the rod, and gather thou the assembly together, thou, and Aaron, thy brother, and speak ye unto the rock before their eyes; and it shall give forth (its) water . . . And Moses took the rod from before the Lord as He commanded him. And Moses and Aaron gathered the congregation together before the rock, and he said unto them, Hear now, ye rebels; must we fetch you water out of this rock? And Moses lifted up his hand, and with his rod he smote the rock twice; and the water came out abundantly, and the congregation drank, and their beasts also. And the Lord spoke unto Moses and Aaron, Because ye believed Me not, to sanctify Me in the eyes of the children of Israel, therefore ye shall not bring this congregation into the land which I have given them. This is the water of Meribah, because the children of Israel strove with the Lord, and he was sanctified in them."

It is unspeakably sad to think of this great man, one of the greatest who ever lived, not being permitted to fulfill his ambition of leading the people of God into the land. We may think his sin was trivial in comparison to that of the rank and file of the people, who sinned so grievously and so frequently. But Moses' sin was great because he was great. That which we regard as small sins, in great men have tremendous consequences. The higher one is elevated by God, the greater will be the fall if failure takes place.

First of all, he spoke unadvisedly with his lips (Ps. 106:33). Losing his self-control, he called God's people, "Ye rebels. Must we fetch you water out of this rock?" Then he disobeyed God and smote the rock twice instead of speaking to it. He spoiled a type. The once-smitten rock (Ex. 17:6) from which the living water flowed, must not be smitten again. The uplifted rock—prefiguring the risen Christ to whom we may speak and from whom our blessings flow—was smitten twice, thus spoiling the intended type. Therein lay Moses' sin for which he was to die. The death and the burial of Moses is described in Deuteronomy 34:

"And Moses went up from the plains of Moab unto the mountain of Nebo, to the top of Pisgah, that is over against Jericho. And the Lord showed him all the land of Gilead, unto Dan. And all Naphtali, and the land of Ephraim, and Manasseh, and all the land of Judah, unto the uttermost sea. And the Negev, and the plain of the valley of Jericho, the city of palm trees, unto Zoar. And the Lord said unto him, This is the land which I swore unto Abraham, unto Isaac, and unto Jacob, saying, I will give it unto thy seed: I have caused thee to see it with thine eyes, but thou shalt not go over there.

So Moses, the servant of God, died there in the land of Moab, according to the word of the Lord. And He buried him in a valley in the land of Moab, over against Beth-peor, but no man knoweth of his sepulcher unto this day."

THE BURIAL OF MOSES

By Nebo's lonely mountain, on this side Jordan's wave,
In a vale in the land of Moab there lies a lonely grave.
But no man dug that sepulcher, and no man saw it e'er,
For the angels of God upturned the sod and laid the dead man there.
That was the grandest funeral that ever passed on earth;
But no man heard the tramping, or saw the train go forth;
Noiselessly as the daylight comes when the night is done,
And the crimson streak on ocean's cheek grows into the great sun.
Lo! when the warrior dieth, his comrades in the war,
With arms reversed and muffled drum, follow the funeral car.
They show the banners taken, and tell his battles won,
And after him lead his masterless steed, while peals the minute gun.
This was the bravest warrior that ever buckled sword;
This the most gifted poet that ever breathed a word;
And never earth's philosopher traced, with his golden pen
On the deathless page truths half so sage as he wrote down for men.
O lonely tomb in Moab's land! O dark Beth-peor's hill !
Speak to these curious hearts of ours, and teach them to be still.
God hath His mysteries of grace, ways that we cannot tell,
He hides them deep, like the secret sleep, of him he loved so well.

—Mrs. C. F. Alexander

4
Caleb & Mount Hebron

The Faithful Follower

In the history of the conquest of the land of Canaan by the Israelites, recorded in the books of Numbers and Joshua, the name of Caleb is outstanding. He and Joshua are the prominent leaders. Joshua is a picture of Christ, and Caleb, as his second-in-command, is a devoted, loyal collaborator. He is an example of the faithful follower of Christ today.

The name Caleb means "a dog," or "wholehearted." To the oriental mind, the word might have a disparaging meaning, but to Westerners the dog is man's best friend and calls to mind many a story of devotedness and loyalty to its master.

The name of Caleb is mentioned for the first time in Numbers 13:6. From the desert of Paran, Moses sent a man of each tribe to spy out the land of Canaan. Among these twelve we find Caleb, the son of Jephunneh, and Hoshea, the son of Nun, whom Moses called Jehoshua (vv. 6, 16). From that moment the two men are closely linked together (see Num. 14:30, 38; 26:65; 34:17-19; Deut. 1:36, 38; Josh. 14:13). The great name of Joshua overshadowed that of Caleb, but throughout the whole campaign of war and conquest, there is no suggestion of jealousy or discontent on the part of Caleb. He was loyal to his commander-in-chief till the end.

It is worthy of note that Caleb was chosen to represent the tribe of Judah when the twelve men were sent to search the land. But on a number of occasions, he is called the Kenezite (Num. 32:12; Josh. 14:6, 14). Kenaz, his ancestor, was the fifth son of Eliphaz, the son of Esau (Gen. 36:11). Apparently a part of the clan of Kenaz had voluntarily associated themselves with the tribe of Judah. It would appear that a so-called outsider became the tribe's chosen representative when courage and initiative were essential.

THE SPY MISSION

The twelve men, chosen for this difficult and dangerous task of surveying the land they were to invade, were the heads and rulers of their respective tribes (Num. 13:2). Today they would be called intelligence agents—spy is not a nice word. In wartime, a person caught in that kind of work would be executed. The Canaanites were a wicked, blood-thirsty people, and their worship showed that they had little regard for human life. The twelve men literally took their lives into their own hands. They had their instructions and, setting out from Kadesh-barnea in the wilderness of Paran, they entered the land by way of the Negev and penetrated as far as Rehob, which ancient maps show to be in the Lebanon area (v. 21).

Only two places are selected for special mention—Hebron and the Brook Eschol. Hebron was an ancient city, built seven years before Zoan in Egypt (Num. 13:22). It was inhabited by three sons of Anak, the people "great and tall" (Deut. 9:2). The other place was Eschol, where they cut a cluster of grapes which it took two men to carry. After spending forty days on the spy mission, they came back to Kadesh-barnea and reported their findings.

Ten of the men gave a pessimistic account of what they had seen. They felt like grasshoppers in the presence of the giant Anakim, so they concluded they never would be able to overcome and dislodge them. It was true that it was a land flowing with milk and honey, but the people were strong, having walled cities and, moreover, they had seen the children of Anak there! As a result, the mass of the people wept and said they were sorry that they ever left Egypt. They talked of organizing a movement to return there.

At this critical point, Caleb stepped in and stilled the people before Moses, and said: "Let us go up at once, and possess it, for we are well able to overcome it." Joshua too intervened, saying, "The land which we passed through to search it, is a very good land. If the Lord delight in us, then He will bring us into this land . . . only rebel not ye against the Lord, neither fear ye the people of the land . . . the Lord is with us, fear them not." But all the congregation demanded to stone them with stones. And the glory of the Lord appeared in the tabernacle of the congregation before all the children of Israel."

As a result of the rebellion of the people, the Lord acted in judgment. All the children twenty years old and under would be spared, but the adults would not be allowed to enter the land. The spies had spent forty days in searching the land, the rebels would spend forty years, a year for a day, of wandering in the wilderness until they were all exterminated. The only survivors would be Caleb and Joshua, the men of faith who trusted God in spite of the difficulties.

The book of Numbers records the history of those sad years of God's hand of judgment on the unbelievers. The first ten chapters give a beautiful outline of the camp of Israel, with the tabernacle in the midst and the twelve tribes gathered around it, with the inner circle of priests and Levites. A census is taken of the men of war. All is set to follow the pillar cloud as it guides them on the comparatively short journey to the Promised Land.

Alas, it was not to be. The crisis came with the evil report of the ten spies at Kadesh-barnea and the sentence of death on the malcontents. The central part of the book records the murmuring, rebellion, and mutiny against the leadership of Moses and Aaron and God's judgment on the rebels. At the end of the book (ch. 26), there was another census: "These are they that were numbered by Moses and Eleazar, the priest, who numbered the children of Israel in the plains of Moab by Jordan near Jericho. But among these there was not a man of them whom Moses and Aaron the priest numbered, when they numbered the children of Israel in the wilderness of Sinai. For the Lord had said of them, They shall surely die in the wilderness. And there was not left a man of them, save Caleb, the son of Jephunneh, and Joshua the son of Nun" (vv. 63-65). At least 603,548 had died in the wilderness (Num. 1:46). After forty years, Caleb and Joshua were the only survivors.

THE CONQUEST

The book of Joshua records the invasion of the Promised Land of Canaan and its distribution among the twelve tribes of Israel. Joshua was the successor of Moses and the God-appointed leader. The tribe of Judah spearheaded the invading troops and Caleb was the recognized head of the tribe. Forty-five years previously on the spy mission, he had seen Hebron for the first time. The place had made a lasting impression on him. In the long years of waiting, he must have dreamed about it again and again. Hebron had a long history. The first time it is mentioned in the Bible is Genesis 13:18. God had made a covenant with Abraham concerning his seed and the land. His seed would be as the dust of the earth and the land—north, south, east, and west—would be his and for his posterity. "Then Abram removed his tent and came and dwelt by the oaks of Mamre which is in Hebron, and built there an altar unto the Lord" (v. 18). Later it was the burial place of Abraham, Sarah, Isaac, Jacob, and Leah—a sacred spot indeed for a devout man like Caleb.

The former name of Hebron was Kirjath-arba (the town of

Arba) Arba was the father of Anak whose family were the giants expelled by Caleb (Josh. 15:13).

THE LONG-CHERISHED HOPE REALIZED (JOSH. 14:6-14)

"Then the children of Judah came unto Joshua in Gilgal, and Caleb the son of Jephunneh the Kenezite, said unto him, Thou knowest the thing that the Lord said unto Moses, the man of God concerning me and thee in Kadesh-barnea. Forty years old was I when Moses, the servant of the Lord, sent me to spy out the land; and I brought him word again as it was in my heart. Nevertheless my brethren who went up with me made the heart of the people melt, but I wholly followed the Lord my God. And Moses swore unto me that day saying, Surely the land whereon thy feet have trodden shall be thine inheritance, and thy children's forever, because thou hast wholly followed the Lord my God. And now, behold the Lord hath kept me alive, as He said, these forty and five years, even since the Lord spoke this word unto Moses, while Israel wandered in the wilderness; and now, lo, I am this day fourscore and five years old. As yet I am as strong this day as I was in the day that Moses sent me; as my strength was then, even so is my strength now, for war, both to go out, and to come in. Now therefore, *give me this mountain,* of which the Lord spoke in that day; for thou heardest in that day how the Anakim were there, and that the cities were great and fortified; if so be the Lord will be with me, then I shall be able to drive them out as the Lord said. And Joshua blessed him, and gave unto Caleb, the son of Jephunneh, Hebron for an inheritance. Hebron, therefore, became the inheritance of Caleb, the son of Jephunneh, the Kenezite, unto this day, because he wholly followed the Lord God of Israel."

There was a promise, but for its fulfillment—that meant a fight. Here was a man, eighty-five years old, willing to attack a stronghold on top of a mountain occupied by a family of giants. But fortified by the knowledge that God was with him, in simple faith he undertook the task. "And Caleb drove out from there the three sons of Anak; Sheshai, and Ahiman, and Talmai, the children of Anak" (Josh. 15:14). A simple statement, with no details. God said to take it, and he did.

Not only did he conquer the central citadel, but he was anxious to secure the surrounding area as well. Debir, formerly called Kirjath-sepher, was about thirteen miles from Hebron. "And Caleb said, He that smiteth Kirjath-sepher, and taketh it, to him will I give Achsah, my daughter in marriage. And Othniel, the son of Kenaz, the brother of Caleb, took it, and he gave him Achsah his daughter in marriage."

The example of the zeal and courage of the old man was an incentive and inspiration to his brother. At the marriage, according to the ancient custom, Achsah asked her father for a blessing. He had given her a southland (the Negev), apparently a dry area. Her request was for springs of water. Then he gave her the upper springs and the lower springs.

"Achsah wanted what would make the southland fruitful; not an exchange, but an addition. So her father gave her 'the upper springs and the nether springs.' In the former we may see a suggestion of the heavenly source of all true blessings; in the latter, the humility required to stoop and enjoy them. We need both and the Lord graciously provides both. All our springs are in Him (Ps. 87:7)." (Carl Armerding)

The story of Caleb and his conquest of the stronghold of Hebron at eighty-five years of age is a tremendous encouragement to elderly servants of God who have arrived at the eventide of life. He lived in a dark day, surrounded by unbelief—people dying every day under God's hand of judicial judgment. But he refused to be discouraged and, with simple faith in the God who keeps His promises, he had a glorious and triumphant old age.

Psalms 90 and 91 would seem to be a commentary on the life and times of Caleb. Psalm 90 was written by Moses, the man of God. It is pessimistic and describes the sad story of the wilderness when a whole generation died on account of their sin and unbelief. It ends with a sevenfold prayer.

Psalm 91, on the other hand, is full of optimism. It commences with a fourfold protection in the secret place of the Most High. Then it continues with a description of preservation from ten perils of the wilderness, and ends with a sevenfold promise, including long life, honor, and salvation. Without stretching our imagination, the psalm could be applied to the experiences of Joshua and Caleb, the heroes of courage and faith at the conquest of Canaan. Verses 11-13 are the great messianic passage, misquoted by Satan at the temptation of our Lord in another desert at the commencement of His public ministry. He too gloriously overcame the barbs of the adversary by using the sword of the Spirit, the Word of God.

5
David & Mount Zion

The Measure of a King

The name of David is mentioned in the Bible 1120 times in 26 books, more frequently than any other human character. His career occupies 58 chapters and the whole of 2 Samuel. He is the author of at least 73 psalms. He is a many-sided character: shepherd, soldier, statesman, sovereign, sufferer, musician, friend, lover. He is the model for all the subsequent kings of Israel. All are measured with him, either like or unlike him. His greatness consisted of a virile manhood with a tender heart. This is always attractive and admirable. "Thy gentleness hath made me great" could be written over his life. The story of David is acknowledged to be "The Historical Masterpiece of the Old Testament."

HIS ANCESTRY (RUTH 4:18-22)

The importance of this small list of names is to show that in the dark days of the Judges, God had not forgotten His sovereign purpose in the preservation of the Messianic line. The meaning of the ten names ending in David are all significant. Ruth the Moabitess had the great distinction of being the great-grandmother of David and of being included in the genealogy of the Messiah (Matt. 1:5-6). Her faith, devotion, and loyalty were abundantly rewarded. Ruth's genealogy has been called "God's highway to Jesus."

David's Life

David's life is seen in two distinct stages: His *rejection* in 1 Samuel and his *reign* in 2 Samuel. One is the counterpart of the other. 1 Samuel records the transition of theocracy to monarchy. Theocratic government under Joshua was the high-water mark of Israel's history. On the death of Joshua and his associates came departure. The period of the Judges was marked by spiritual and moral decline. The first part of 1 Samuel centers around three persons: Eli the priest, Samuel the prophet, and Saul the king. Failure to a greater or lesser degree characterized all three. The sovereign rule of Jehovah had been rejected and man's rule substituted for it. Eli died of a broken neck when he heard of the capture of the ark by the Philistines; Samuel the prophet, God's "Emergency Man" (W. W. Fereday), had an impeccable record of faithfulness, but his family was no improvement on Eli's. As for Saul, he was a complete failure.

It was at this point that God stepped in. Samuel was sent to Bethlehem to the home of Jesse, where David, his youngest son, was anointed as king in the midst of his brethren. This is the first of three anointings of David as king: first, in Bethlehem (1 Sam. 16:13); secondly, over the royal tribe of Judah (2 Sam. 2:4); and thirdly, over all the twelve tribes of Israel at Hebron (2 Sam. 5:3).

The Period of Rejection (1 Sam. 16-31). Basically David's trouble and exile at this time resulted from the envy and jealousy of King Saul. The incident of the slaying of the giant, Goliath of Gath (ch. 17), and the song of the women, "Saul hath slain his thousands and David his ten thousands," brought matters to a head. Saul had given David his younger daughter Michal to be his wife and invited him to sit at his table in the royal palace. But while David played the harp in his presence, seeking to calm his overwrought passions, Saul on two occasions tried to take his life by casting a javelin at him. "Love is strong as death, jealousy is cruel as the grave; its coals are coals of fire, which have a most vehement flame."

David experienced both love and hate in the home of Saul. Ironically, one of David's best friends and admirers was Jonathan, Saul's son and possible heir. He knew that David was destined to be the king instead of his father, yet there was no envy or jealousy on his part. The relationship between David and Jonathan is one of the most beautiful in Scripture. After the second attempt on his life and a warning by Jonathan, David had no other alternative but to flee. Alas, Jonathan stayed with his demon-crazed father to the end and died with him.

In the meantime, David, as a fugitive and hunted exile, gathered a band of loyal followers around him. One of his strongholds was the cave Adullam.

They were a mixed and, on the surface at least, not an encouraging crowd to depend on. "And every one who was in distress, and every one who was in debt, and every one who was discontented, gathered themselves unto him; and he became a captain over them; and there were with him about four hundred men." It speaks well for David as a leader and for them as soldiers that deeds of valor and loyalty were performed by them which were suitably rewarded when David was in prosperity on the throne as king. But in the meantime there was discouragement, depression, and doubt. There was a lapse of faith, when he took his family to Moab for shelter and when he went to Gath, the Philistine stronghold, and pretended to be mad.

Saul and his men of war followed him relentlessly with the object of taking David's life. Many of his experiences at this time are recorded in the Psalms. Psalms 57 and 142 were written when he was in the cave (see also inscriptions to Psalms 52, 54, and 56). These poetic compositions throw a floodlight on his spiritual exercises and feelings. David's long-drawn-out exile and rejection ended with the death of Saul and his son Jonathan at the hands of the Philistines, as recorded in 1 Samuel 31. David's elegy at their death (2 Sam. 1:17-27) is one of the most beautiful passages in human language.

David anointed as king. After the death of Saul, there was an abortive attempt to make his son Ish-bosheth king over the northern tribes. This only lasted for two years. At the end, he was assassinated by two of his servants. But David, instructed by God, went to Hebron where he was anointed king over the royal tribe of Judah. After the death of Ish-bosheth and the collapse of the kingdom of the house of Saul, "all the elders of Israel came to the king at Hebron; and King David made a league with them in Hebron before the Lord, and they anointed David king over Israel. David was thirty years old when he began to reign and he reigned forty years. In Hebron he reigned over Judah seven years and six months; and in Jerusalem he reigned thirty and three years over all Israel and Judah" (2 Sam. 5:3-5).

The Capture of Jerusalem (2 Sam. 5:6-10). The first mention of Jerusalem in the Bible is in Genesis 14:18. There it is called Salem, the city of peace (Heb. 7:2). The historic Melchizedek, whose name means "king of righteousness," was its king-priest. The writer of the Epistle to the Hebrews has a lot to say about him as a type of the Lord Jesus.

The next reference is in Joshua 15:63, "As for the Jebusites, the inhabitants of Jerusalem, the children of Judah could not drive them out; but the Jebusites dwell with the children of Judah at Jerusalem unto this day." A later reference is in Judges 1:8, "Now the children of Judah had fought against Jerusalem, and had taken it, and smitten it with the edge of the sword, and set the city on fire." Then in verse 21, we read, "And the children of Benjamin did not drive out the Jebusites, who inhabited Jerusalem, but the Jebusites dwell with the children of of Benjamin in Jerusalem unto this day." Apparently the Jebusites were a strong, stubborn people and they controlled the city of Jerusalem until David's day.

In approximately 1000 BC, David came from Hebron in command of the united armies of all Israel and camped before Jerusalem. Thinking that their stronghold was impregnable, the Jebusites mocked the Hebrew army by placing on the walls the lame and the blind as a defense force. While David's main army made a frontal attack on the city, his general, Joab, and his assistants crept up through the vertical watershaft west of the Gihon Spring, surprised the garrison and took the city. King David made it his capital and renamed it Mount Zion. This was all in God's purpose and plan. It was to be the center both of goverment and worship as far as Israel was concerned. The tabernacle with a decadent priesthood and without the ark of the covenant was now in obscurity at Shiloh. But all of this was to be changed. "Moreover He refused the tabernacle of Joseph, and chose not the tribe of Ephraim. But chose the tribe of Judah, the Mount Zion which He loved. And He built His sanctuary like high palaces, like the earth which He hath established forever. He chose David also His servant, and took him from the sheepfolds; from following the ewes great with young, He brought him to feed Jacob His people, and Israel His inheritance. So He fed them according to the integrity of His heart, and guided them by the skillfulness of His hands" (Ps. 78:67-72). This is a dramatic turning point in the history of Israel.

David and the Ark of the Covenant. Psalm 132 describes an early experience in David's life. At his home in Bethlehem, he had heard of the capture of the ark of the covenant by the Philistines, and of its present location in the home of Abinadab at Kirjath-jearim (The Field of the Wood, Ps. 132:6; 1 Sam. 7:1-2). He determined that he would not build his own house until he had a suitable resting place for the ark as the symbol of God's presence among His gathered people. After he was crowned king and installed in the capital at Jerusalem, this was his first priority. The thrilling story of how his youthful vow was fulfilled is told in 2 Samuel 6:12-19. A number of Psalms seem to be associated with this joyful and important event, e.g., Ps. 24; 68; 78; 132. It is also a most important landmark in the history of the worship of Jehovah by the nation of Israel.

Having 'found' the ark, David, being divinely directed, did not return it to the forsaken tabernacle at Shiloh, but eventually brought it to God's new center (2 Sam. 6:17; 2 Chron. 1:4). Jehovah's dwelling place was now Zion (Ps. 76:2; 132:13). When David brought the ark to Jerusalem and placed it in a tent which he had pitched for it, a unique period of worship was initiated. This lasted for thirty years, until the temple was built in the reign of Solomon. The scene is described in 1 Chronicles 15:25 to 16.3 (RV): "So David and the elders of Israel, and the captains over thousands, went to bring up the ark of the covenant of the Lord out of the house of Obededom with joy; and it came to pass, when God helped the Levites that bare the ark of the covenant of the Lord, that they sacrificed seven bullocks and seven rams. And David was clothed with a robe of fine linen, and all the Levites that bare the ark, and the singers, and Chenaniah the master of song with the singers; and David had upon him an ephod of linen ... And they brought in the ark of God, and set it in the midst of the tent that David had pitched for it; and they offered burnt offerings and peace offerings before God. And when David had made an end of offering the burnt offerings and the peace offerings, he blessed the people in the name of the Lord. And he dealt to every one of Israel, both man and woman, to everyone a loaf of bread, and a good piece of flesh, and a cake of raisins. And he appointed certain of the Levites to minister before the ark of the Lord, and to celebrate, and to thank and praise the Lord, the God of Israel."

In this unique period of transition, David the king is seen dressed in a priestly ephod and offering sacrifices of burnt offerings and peace offerings. A new order of service is instituted in which the Levites are appointed to a praise ministry before the ark (1 Chron. 16:4). The sacrifices here were for thanksgiving, not like the sin offering in the now abandoned tabernacle, where the blood was formerly sprinkled on the golden lid of the ark, on the Day of Atonement. David's tent was a temporary arrangement which awaited the building of God's house, the temple. But the amazing thing is that David functioned as a priest on this occasion, and was able to go into the presence of God without any intervening veil. We know that David was a prophet (Acts 2:30), and a king. On bringing up the ark to its temporary resting place, wearing a priestly ephod and offering blood sacrifices, he foreshadows our Lord Jesus Christ as prophet, priest, and king.

THE DAVIDIC COVENANT (2 SAM. 7:16; PS. 89:3-4, 34, 37)

As soon as he had established his kingdom and throne on Mount Zion and the country had rest from war, David's first priority was to fulfill his longtime ambition to build a temple, a permanent place of worship. He mentioned this to his friend, Nathan the prophet, who encouraged him in the project. But then God intervened. David was a man of war: the building of the temple must wait for his son, Solomon, who was a man of peace. Instead, God made David a promise and outlined a covenant with him which was unconditional and everlasting. Its importance cannot be overemphasized. It concerned a seed, a house, a throne, and a kingdom which would be established forever. It was confirmed by a divine oath (Ps. 89:35). David's descendants might fail and fall into grievous sins. We know they did. This would be dealt with in righteous judgment, but would not annul the covenant. In his last words, David could say, "Although my house be not so with God, yet He hath made with me an everlasting covenant, ordered in all things and sure; for this is all my salvation, and all my desire" (2 Sam. 23:5).

Looking back from our vantage point in time, we can see how the covenant promises have been fulfilled. The covenant culminated in the coming of the Messiah through the kings of Judah. The "seed" was the promised seed of the woman fulfilled in the Incarnation of our Lord Jesus Christ, the son of David, the son of Abraham (Matt. 1:1; Lk. 1:69). Looking forward to His coming again in glory, we are confident that the house, the throne, and the everlasting kingdom will also be fulfilled (Isa. 32-33; Jer. 33:19-22; Ezek. 40-48).

DAVID'S GREAT SIN AND ITS CONSEQUENCES
(2 SAM. 11-12; Ps. 32; Ps. 51)

One of the most pathetic statements concerning David's life is 1 Kings 15:5, "Because David did that which was right in the eyes of the Lord, and turned not aside from anything that he commanded him all the days of his life, except only in the matter of Uriah, the Hittite." After the events of Elah, Adullam, Hebron, and Mount Zion, he could have rested on his triumphs.

He was the author of the 23rd Psalm and was the "man after God's own heart." Instead of being spiritually alert, his guard was down. While his army was fighting a crucial battle in Trans-Jordan, he was having a siesta on the rooftop of his home in Jerusalem. Arising from his rest and looking over the patios of the homes in the city, he saw a woman, Bath-sheba. Her husband, Uriah, was fighting with the army in Amman. The floodtides of passion were unloosed and David committed three sins: first, adultery with the woman; then, by a stratagem, he was responsible for the death of Uriah her husband; and thirdly, he tried to cover up what he had done. Altogether it was a capital crime which, under law, merited the death penalty.

After an interval in which David suffered agonies of remorse (Ps. 32:3-4), God sent Nathan the prophet to him. He told him the parable of the rich man who took and slaughtered a desperately poor man's pet lamb to provide a feast for a visiting guest. On hearing this, David impulsively burst out, "As the Lord liveth, the man that has done this shall surely die; and he shall restore the lamb fourfold, because he did this thing, and because he had no pity." Nathan responded, "David, thou art the man!"

David's genuine repentance is recorded in Psalm 51 and his gracious forgiveness by God in Psalm 32, but sins of this type, although forgiven and the person is restored, yet in God's governmental dealings with his children, there are always serious repercussions in the subsequent life. David was told that the sword would never depart from his house. He himself had declared that the man that had no pity would restore fourfold. He had the sad, heartbreaking experience of seeing this in his own sons and family circle. It is still true that "God is not mocked: for whatsoever a man soweth, that shall he also reap" (Gal. 6:7).

DAVID AND MOUNT ZION

Zion is mentioned more than any other mountain in Scripture. It has geographical, historical, political, prophetical, and spiritual significance. The name is used most often in Isaiah and the Psalms. It was the best fortified mountain of Jerusalem, with deep valleys on three sides. It was selected and conquered by David as his citadel and capital of his kingdom. It was also chosen by God as the gathering center of His people, the site for the building of the temple. Prophetically it is destined to be the metropolis of the millennial earth, from which the King of Glory will rule and reign (Ps. 2:6; 48:1-2). Spiritually it is contrasted with Mount Sinai, the place of rigid law, fire, smoke, and judgment. Instead, Mount Zion symbolizes rest, home, peace, righteous government, and protection. David and his men must not have known or dreamed of the glorious future which lay ahead as they climbed the watershaft and captured the stronghold of Zion (2 Sam. 5:6-10).

ADDENDUM

David's Mount Zion should not be confused with the mountain in Old Jerusalem which now bears that name. The city straddles four hills which are defined by three main valleys: the Kidron on the east, the Tyropoeon (Cheesemakers) running approximately north and south through the center of the city, and the Hinnom on the west and south. These three valleys meet southeast of the city at the En Rogel Spring.

Of the four hills, the southeastern hill was the first inhabited, no doubt due to the Gihon Spring on its eastern flank and its defensibility, surrounded as it is by valleys. This was the ancient Salem where Melchizedek lived, the Jebus that David captured. This narrow ridge is less than 200 feet wide at the the top and covers no more than eight acres. When Suleiman rebuilt the walls of the city in 1537, this Zion was left outside the ramparts.

As the city spread north onto Moriah during Solomon's reign, and west onto the southwestern hill, the meaning of Zion expanded to encompass these three, and perhaps Olivet as well—"the *mountains* of Zion" (Ps. 133:3). For some reason, the name now has migrated to mean only the southwestern hill, not the southeastern, as in David's day.

6
Elijah & Mount Carmel

The Measure of a King

Elijah has been called "the Prophet of Fire." He appears suddenly in Scripture with the mere mention of his name. Like Melchizedek, nothing is known of his parentage or upbringing. As Melchizedek is a type of the king-priest, Elijah is the typical prophet with a message from God. His name incorporates two great titles of God: *El*, the Almighty Creator, and *Jah*, the Covenant-keeping One. He must have had godly, enlightened parents to give him such a majestic name. He is called the Tishbite who was of the inhabitants of Gilead. This was in the tribal area of Manasseh and Gad, east of the Jordan. Gilead was a wild country of high mountains, deep valleys, shaggy forests, mountain torrents, and wild beasts. Like John the Baptist, he is one of the few men whose personal appearance is described in Holy Scripture. The Authorized Version pictures him as "an hairy man and girded with a girdle of leather about his waist (2 Kings 1:8). But the RSV translates it, "He wore a garment of haircloth, and a girdle of leather about his loins." Also the JND (New) Translation has it, "He was a man in a hairy (garment), and girt with a girdle of leather about his loins." The meaning is correctly given as that of "a man with a garment of hair," that is, a garment made of goats' or camels' hair, dark and shaggy. This garb is elsewhere called his "mantle." With it he covered his face when he saw the glory of God at Horeb (1 Kings 19:13), and with it he smote the waters of Jordan so that he and Elisha went over on dry ground (2 Kings 2:8). His appearance would be in complete contrast to the cultured courtiers of Samaria who would regard him as the wild man from Gilead. He is the great example of a man with an obscure background and a rugged personality whom God in His sovereignty chooses at a critical point in human history to head up a revival. God, in His infinite wisdom, knows the type of man that is needed in any particular situation. Moses was an intellectual, "learned in all the wisdom of the Egyptians," the leader chosen to deliver Israel from Egyptian bondage. But Elijah, the stranger from Gilead, was God's choice to arrest apostasy.

"In some respects, Elijah was unique among the Old Testament prophets. He was the first to raise a dead person, and he passed out of the world without tasting death; he left an immediate successor behind him in Elisha, and he had a moral successor in John the Baptist (Lk. 1:17; Matt. 17:12). Moreover, Elijah was sent back to earth with Moses to do honor to the Lord Jesus on the Mount of Transfiguration; and his work is even yet unfinished. His voice will be heard again in Israel (Mal. 4:5)." (W. W. Fereday)

THE CONDITION OF ISRAEL

When Elijah appeared, it was fifty-eight years since the kingdom was divided by Jeroboam. Since David's reign, there had been five reforming kings in the southern kingdom in Jerusalem. But in this brief period there had been seven kings in the northern kingdom of Israel, whose capital was in Samaria. Without exception they were wicked men. In Elijah's day, the king of Israel living in his royal palace at Samaria was the weak-kneed Ahab, dominated by his arrogant wife, Jezebel, who has been called "the worst woman in Holy Scripture." She had a pagan background and a reputation of persecuting anything that savored of loyalty to Jehovah and His people. It was to this ungodly and graceless pair that Elijah first appeared with a ringing message from God: "As Jehovah, the God of Israel, liveth, before whom I stand, there shall not be dew nor rain these years, but according to my word" (1 Kings 17:1). It was abrupt and devastating, but Elijah did not act on his own initiative. Elijah was a man who knew his Bible, he knew his God, and was a man of fervent prayer. He was doubtless familiar with the words of Deuteronomy 11:16-17, "Take heed to yourselves, that your heart be not deceived, and ye turn aside, and serve other gods, and worship them; and Jehovah's wrath be kindled against you, and He shut up the heaven that there be no rain, and that the land yield not her fruit; and ye perish quickly from off the good land which Jehovah giveth you."

With these words burning in his brain, he went into God's presence and prayed, "O God, stop the rain." God heard his cry and responded to his faith and "it rained not on the earth by the space of three years and six months." The worship of Baal was a debased worship of the sun-god. It was a fitting chastisement. For three-and-a-half years, the worshipers were exposed to the fierce, scorching rays of their deity. The time of the judgment probably has a prophetic significance. In the book of Revelation, it is the time of one-half of the prophetic week, the period of the Great Tribulation. Revelation 11:6 describes two witnesses who prophesy during that period, and who have power to shut heaven. The reference seems to refer to Elijah as being one of them.

CHERITH

"And the word of the Lord came unto him saying, Get thee hence, and turn thee eastward, and hide thyself by the brook Cherith, that is before Jordan. And it shall be, that thou shalt drink of the brook; and I have commanded the ravens to feed thee there. So he went and did according to the word of the Lord . . . And the ravens brought him bread and flesh in the morning and bread and flesh in the evening, and he drank of the brook."

"The word of the Lord came." This is the second time God speaks. Elijah can have no doubt about the will of the Lord for his pathway. He also has God's promise for the supply of his daily needs. Cherith was probably east of Jordan, towards the sunrising in Elijah's own country. It was to be a time of preparation, waiting, and testing in his native land. This is God's method with His chosen servants. We are reminded of John the Baptist and Paul in Arabia and Tarsus. To be in the backside of the desert, dependent on God for daily needs, is not wasted time. For Elijah, Cherith was the school of faith in God for his very existence, but he was not disappointed. As he watched the drying brook, the direct result of his own stand for God, he had the consolation that God had sent him there. God had said, "The ravens shall feed thee there." There is strong emphasis on the word *there.* The ravens were God's liveried servants. Impure by nature and Sinaitic law (Lev. 11:15), the ravens are so voracious that, if God did not intervene, they would allow their young to starve (Job 38:41). Yet here they miraculously deny themselves to feed Elijah. The ravens and the brook, were a combination of the supernatural and the natural. It was the latter that gave out first. No saint need worry about the natural, as long as the supernatural is in operation. In these last materialistic days, George Muller practised and taught the church the great truth of simple faith and trust in God for daily needs to carry on the work of God. Is not our God the God of Elijah?

ZAREPHATH

At Cherith, his faith for the daily supply of food and drink—the necessities of life—was tested. He was alone with

God in that test, but at Zarephath his temperament in relation with other people was tested. This is very important in the life of a servant of God. Sarepta (as it is called in Luke 4:26) was on the public road between Tyre and Sidon. The Lord had said: "Arise, get thee to Zarephath, which belongeth to Zidon, and dwell there; behold, I have commanded a widow woman to sustain thee" (1 Kings 17:9). This involved a journey of over 100 miles through country where Elijah's name was hated. It was the very heart of the area where Jezebel and her idolatry came from.

He was first tested in his own country at Cherith, then here in the center of heathendom, the country of Eth-Baal. The name Zarephath means, "smelting house," the furnace or workshop for refining of metals. It was to be a refining process for Elijah. When he arrived, he met an old widow woman gathering a few sticks to light a fire and cook what she thought was her last meal. She was on the verge of starvation and the poorest of the poor. It must have been a shock to his pride of independence to be a guest in her house. The only food supply was an almost empty meal barrel and a practically dry cruse of oil. Then Elijah made an amazing request. "Make me a little cake first, and afterwards for thee and thy son." This was not arrogant selfishness, for he immediately added, "For thus saith the Lord God of Israel, The barrel of meal shall not be used up, neither shall the cruse of oil fail, until the day that the Lord sendeth rain upon the earth."

She went and did according to the word of Elijah, and she and he and her house ate for many days. It was a daily experience to scrape the bottom of the barrel, but the supply was always there. They learned the truth of the Lord's prayer, "Give us this day our daily bread." It was a day-at-a-time experience of dependence on God.

But Elijah had still to face the greatest challenge to his self-control and his faith in God. The widow's son became critically ill and died. In a frenzy, she turned to Elijah and screamed:

"Have you come here to slay my son and bring my sin to re-
membrance?" This was hardly fair, to blame an innocent man
for the death of her child. But it was part of God's discipline
of His servant to know how to take insult and exercise self-
control. In reply, Elijah quietly turned to the mother and said,
"Give me thy son. And he took him out of her bosom, and
carried him up into an upper chamber, and laid him upon his
own bed."

He stretched himself upon the child three times and cried
to the Lord in a brief but remarkable prayer of faith, "O Lord
my God, I pray thee, let this child's soul come unto him
again." And the Lord heard the voice of Elijah, and the soul
of the child came unto him again and he revived. Elijah delivered the child to his mother and said, "See, thy child liveth."
She replied, "Now by this I know that thou art a man of God,
and that the Word of the Lord in thy mouth is truth." Elijah
was now ready for the greatest challenge of his life at Mount
Carmel. His experiences at Cherith, and in the humble home
at Zarephath had fitted him for it.

MOUNT CARMEL

"And it came to pass, after many days that the word of the
Lord came to Elijah in the third year, saying, Go, show thyself
unto Ahab, and I will send rain upon the earth." When Ahab
saw Elijah, he said to him, "Art thou he that troubleth Israel?"
Elijah replied, "I have not troubled Israel, but you and your
father's house, in that you have forsaken the commandments
of the Lord and have followed Baalim. Now therefore send
and gather to me all Israel unto Mount Carmel, and the four
hundred and fifty prophets of Baal, and the four hundred
prophets of the groves that eat at Jezebel's table."

Ahab obligingly sent to all Israel and gathered the
prophets together to Mount Carmel. Then Elijah spoke to the
assembly, "How long halt ye between two opinions? If the
Lord be God, follow Him; but if Baal, follow him." And the

people answered him not a word. What could they say?

The Vital Test of Reality: Baal or Jehovah, who was the Living God? Elijah's proposal to discover the truth was very simple. Two sacrificial bullocks were to be provided, one for the prophets of Baal, the other for himself. Two altars, one for Baal and the other, the ancient altar of Jehovah. The bullocks were to be killed, cut in pieces, and laid on wood on the altars with no fire underneath. The prophets of Baal were to call on the name of their god, and Elijah was to call on the name of Jehovah. The God that answered by fire to consume the sacrifice was the true God.

The people, who believed that Baal was the god of fire, said, "It is well spoken." Elijah gave the prophets of Baal the option of moving first in preparing the bullock and building the altar, but emphasized, "No fire underneath" (1 Kings 18:25). Pagan miracles have a bad reputation for imposture! From morning till noon the prophets cried, "O Baal, answer us," but in the long, continued silence of their god, they went into a frenzy. They leaped on their altar and with swords and knives slashed themselves until the blood flowed. Elijah mocked them, saying that perhaps their god was not at home, had other business, or maybe he was asleep. This continued for three hours longer.

The Time of Sacrifice: At the time of the evening sacrifice, Elijah judged that it was time for him to act. It was the hour when the evening lamb was being sacrificed on the altar in the temple in Jerusalem, prefiguring Christ and His death on the Cross. He silenced the crowd by saying, "Come near unto me." He proceeded to repair the altar of the Lord that was broken down. He took twelve stones according to the number of the tribes of the sons of Jacob, refusing to recognize the divided condition of Israel in his day. With the stones he built an altar in the name of the Lord and dug a trench around it. Then he put the wood in order and cut the bullock in pieces and laid them on the wood. Then he said, "Fill four barrels with water, and pour it on the burnt sacrifice and on the wood." This was repeated three times. The water ran round about the altar and filled the trench.

At the time of the offering of the evening sacrifice, Elijah came near and prayed, saying: "Lord God of Abraham, Isaac and of Israel, let it be known this day that Thou art God in Israel, and that I am Thy servant, and that I have done all these things at Thy word. Hear me, O Lord, hear me, that this people may know that Thou art the Lord God, and that Thou hast turned their heart back again." Then the fire of the Lord fell and consumed the burnt sacrifice, and the wood, and the stones, and the dust, and licked up the water that was in the trench. And when all the people saw it, they fell on their faces and said, "The Lord, He is the God, the Lord He is the God." And Elijah said unto them, "Take the prophets of Baal, let not one of them escape." And they took them, and Elijah brought them down to the brook Kishon and slew them there.

The Sound of Abundance of Rain: After the slaughter of the prophets of Baal, Elijah turned to Ahab and said: "Get thee up, eat and drink; for there is a sound of abundance of rain." But he himself and his servant went to the top of Carmel and cast himself upon the ground and put his face between his knees. He said to his servant, "Go up now, look towards the sea." And he went up and looked and said, "There is nothing." And he said, "Go again" seven times. At the seventh time, he said, "There rises out of the sea a little cloud like a man's hand." And he said, "Go up, say unto Ahab, Prepare thy chariot, that the rain stop thee not."

In the meantime, the heaven was black with clouds and wind and there was a great rain. And Ahab rode and went to Jezreel. And the hand of the Lord was on Elijah, and he girded up his loins and ran before Ahab to the entrance to Jezreel (approximately 18 miles).

The reforming work of Elijah at Mount Carmel was the climax of his mission and ministry. Cherith and Zarephath had prepared him for it and it was brilliantly carried out. Although he was a man of like passions with ourselves, yet this contest demonstrated that he was a man of courage and of prayer. He knew the Word of God and had remarkable faith in its promises. He is an outstanding example of the men that God raises up at a critical time in the history of His chosen people. He was very human and had his difficult experiences of weakness and failure, but we are thankful for the record of his mountaintop triumphs as well as the dark valley through which he passed.

FLIGHT

After his mighty victory at Mount Carmel and his sevenfold prayer for rain, Elijah ran in wild exultation ahead of Ahab's chariot to the entrance of the royal summer palace at Jezreel. He did not go right in to demand the life of Jezebel. Instead, when Ahab informed her of the slaughter of the priests of Baal, she threatened with an oath to behead Elijah within twenty-four hours, as many years later Herodias did with John the Baptist.

Hearing this, Elijah turned and fled for his life, about 100 miles to Beersheba, the southern border of Judah. The place has many memories of Abraham and the patriarchs. He left his servant there and went a further day's march into the wilderness and, completely exhausted, collapsed under a juniper tree, and prayed that he might die. "It is enough, now, O Lord, take away my life, for I am not better than my fathers." The emotional change in such a short time in God's dear servant, from the heights of triumph at Carmel to the depths of depression and discouragement seems incredible. Yet it happens so often, not only in the biblical records but in our own day. We are thankful for the written record of the experience of this hungry, tired, lonely, and discouraged man. Some have passed harsh judgment on Elijah, saying that he deviated from God's purpose in his life by running away at the empty threat of a woman. But God is kinder than that. He said to the weary, distraught servant, "The journey is too great for thee." He was hungry and an angel gave him food and drink. He was exhausted and God gave him a good night's sleep. A good untroubled sleep is the best therapy for a weary man. It is beautiful to see that the meal was specially prepared, "A cake baken on the coals and a cruse of water at his head." We are reminded of One who cooked a meal on the seashore for erring Peter and then spoke to his heart and conscience (Jn. 21:9-19). After the twofold touch of the angel and the word of comfort, he got up and went in the strength of that meal—and the encouraging word—forty days and forty nights to Horeb, the mount of God.

Horeb was a part of the range of mountains of which Sinai was a prominent peak. We do not know what motivated Elijah to take that long journey. Possibly he thought that as Jehovah had revealed Himself to Moses, he too might get a revelation from God there. If so, he was correct in his thought. God did speak in no uncertain way, but not in the same manner as he spoke to Moses. To Moses it was the revelation of inscrutable law accompanied by thunder, lightning, and smoke, but to Elijah it was a revelation of correction, restoration, and recommission accompanied by "a still small voice."

He had hidden himself in a cave and the word of the Lord called to him, "What doest thou here, Elijah?" And he answered, "I have been very jealous for the Lord God of Hosts; for the children of Israel have forsaken thy covenant, thrown down Thy altars, and slain Thy prophets with the edge of the sword, and I, even I only, am left, and they seek my life, to take it away." After this mournful litany, the Lord commanded him to go forth and stand upon the mount. (Here we are forcibly reminded of God's revelation to Moses on the mount, Ex. 33:21-22.) As the Lord passed by, there was a mighty wind, an earthquake, and a fire. But the Lord was not in these. This was followed by a voice of gentle stillness. The Divine self-revelation is usually manifested "in the secret place of the Most High" (Ps. 91:1) as we meditate quietly on the written Word and the Living Word. After hearing the voice, Elijah returned to the cave and, standing at its entrance, wrapped his face in his mantle.

Again God spoke: "What doest thou here, Elijah?" In reply, Elijah repeated his woeful story. He had brooded over it and, like a child in kindergarten, could repeat it by rote. But the last two items were not true. In spite of Jezebel's empty threats, no one was attempting to kill him and above all, he was not alone. The Lord reminded him that there were 7,000 that had not bowed the knee to Baal. Moreover, the Lord had some further work for him to do. He had to anoint two kings and a young man as his successor in the prophetic office, Elisha by name. Instead of answering his prayer under the juniper tree that he might die, God had higher plans for His dear servant. The second chapter of 2 Kings records how he was raptured up to heaven by a chariot of fire and a whirlwind without tasting death.

Elijah is a man of the mountaintop. First of Mount Carmel, then Mount Horeb, and the Mount of Transfiguration (Matt. 17:3). There does not seem any doubt that he will have an important part to play in the coming great and terrible Day of the Lord (Mal. 4:5).

ADDENDUM

Skeptics have found the story of the Battle of the Gods to be incredulous because Elijah instructed the people to pour twelve barrels of water over the altar. How could they find twelve barrels, ask the doubters, when the problem was a great drought? Even a cursory look at a map of the region shows Mount Carmel jutting out into the Mediterranean. This would provide more than enough salt water to pour on the sacrifice, but none to alleviate their thirst.

Part Two
Christ of the Mountaintop

Seven Mountains in Matthew's Gospel

There are seven mountains in Matthew's Gospel associated with Christ:

1) The Mount of Temptation (Matthew 4:1-11);
2) The Mount of Teaching (Matthew 5-7);
3) The Mount of Intercession (Matthew 14);
4) The Mount of Transfiguration (Matthew 17);
5) The Mount of Olives (Matthew 24-25);
6) Mount Calvary (Matthew 27);
7) The Mountain in Galilee (Matthew 28);

These events recorded in the life and ministry of our Lord are linked together and are doctrinally important.

In our former studies, we have been considering six men in the Old Testament whose lives and testimony for God were climaxed on a mountain. All of them were great men of power and accomplishment, but alongside their brilliant victories, there was often a deep valley of failure and defeat. The higher the mountain, the deeper the valley. It is often so with ourselves today. After some spiritual mountaintop experience, we are plunged into a valley of discouragement and depression. But not so our Lord and Master. To Him, seeming defeat ended in glorious triumph and exaltation. "He shall not fail nor be discouraged, till He have set judgment in the earth, and the isles shall wait for His law" (Isa. 42:4). While the six Old Testament men on their mountains may well pre-figure our Lord Jesus Christ, He is the Perfect Servant who set His face as a flint and "who for the joy that was set before Him, endured the cross, despising the shame, and is set down at the right hand of the throne of God" (Heb. 12:2).

We shall now consider the mountaintop experiences of our Lord in Matthew's Gospel.

7
The Mount of Temptation

Matthew 4:1-11

There are two events in the life of our Lord which took place at the beginning of His public ministry. They are closely related: first, His baptism by John at the River Jordan; and immediately after, His temptation by Satan in the wilderness. At His baptism, His divine Person and His messianic mission were authenticated by the voice of God the Father from heaven, "This is My beloved Son, in whom I am well pleased." It was also confirmed by the Holy Spirit, which in bodily shape as a dove descended upon Him (Lk. 3:22). This was His official presentation to Israel, fulfilling Psalm 2:7 and Isaiah 42. In Mark's brief account of the temptation, we read, "And immediately the Spirit driveth Him into the wilderness. And He was there in the wilderness forty days, tempted of Satan; and was with the wild beasts; and the angels ministered unto Him" (Mk. 1:12-13).

There is a distinct parallel and also a contrast between the temptation by Satan of the first man Adam in the Garden of Eden, and the Last Adam—the representative Man—Christ Jesus in the wilderness. The first man, Adam, was in a perfect environment, which ministered to all his physical needs, but the Last Adam, Jesus, had fasted for forty days and was physically weakened by hunger; and He was not in a garden, but in a wilderness where wild beasts roamed. Then Satan used a similar strategy which he had used in Eden. His three temptations were directed to body, soul, and spirit. They were successful in bringing about the Fall of the first man, with all its terrible consequences for the human race. Not so with the second Man, the Last Adam.

THE THREE TEMPTATIONS

The First Temptation: Satan said, "If Thou be the Son of God, command that these stones be made bread." The Lord Jesus responded, "It is written, Man shall not live by bread alone, but by every word that proceedeth out of the mouth of God" (Deut. 8:3-4). This temptation was directed to His body, the desire of the flesh.

The Second Temptation: The devil took Him up to Jerusalem, and set Him on a pinnacle of the temple. There he said to Him, "If Thou be the Son of God, cast Thyself down; for it is written, He shall give His angels charge concerning Thee: and in their hands they shall bear Thee up, lest at any time Thou dash Thy foot against a stone." Jesus responded, "It is written again, Thou shalt not tempt the Lord thy God" (Deut. 6:16).

In this temptation, Satan misquoted Psalm 91:11-12. He left out "to keep Thee in all Thy ways." It was to do something spectacular in order to attract the crowd. It was directed to the soul, emotions, the pride of life.

The Third Temptation: Again the devil taketh Him up into an exceeding high mountain, and showeth Him all the kingdoms of the world and the glory of them. And said unto Him: "All these things will I give Thee if Thou wilt fall down and worship me." Luke 4:6-7 adds: "All this power will I give Thee, and the glory of them, for that is delivered unto me; and to whomsoever I will give it. If Thou therefore wilt worship me, all shall be Thine."

Then said Jesus unto him, "Get thee hence, Satan, for it is

written, Thou shalt worship the Lord thy God, and Him only shalt thou serve" (quoting Deut. 6:13).

This climactic temptation was aimed at His Spirit, and the sight of His eyes. And when the devil had ended the temptation "for a season," he departed from Him (Lk. 4:13) and angels came and ministered to Him.

This was just the beginning of a series of attacks by Satan on our Lord which came to a head on the Cross. Paul describes that attack and the victory of the Saviour in these words: "And having spoiled principalities and powers, He made a show of them openly, triumphing over them in it" (Col. 2:15).

The doctrinal signification of the temptation of Christ and His victory over Satan at the beginning of His public ministry is most important. The view is propagated by some in evangelical circles that the representative Man, Jesus, was tempted in the realm of His human nature, and in that sense He could have sinned, otherwise there was no point in the temptation or test. The error here is in separating the human nature from the divine nature of our Lord Jesus Christ. He was God manifest in the flesh (1 Tim. 3:16). Two passages in the Epistle to the Hebrews speak of His temptation: "For in that He hath suffered being tempted, He is able to succour them that are tempted" (2:18); and again, "For we have not an high priest which cannot be touched with the feeling of our infirmities; but was in all points tempted like as we are, yet without sin" (4:15). Thank God He is both sinless and impeccable.

There is one practical lesson we should learn from the manner in which our Lord overcame the temptations of Satan. It was His use of the sword of the Spirit, the living Word of God. The threefold quotation from a small section of the book of Deuteronomy was sufficient to demolish and overthrow the attacks of the enemy. In this day of satanic and demon activity, it is imperative to study, memorize, and meditate on the Word of God—not only to have the sword in the scabbard, but be able to wield it effectually when the enemy strikes.

8
The Mount of Teaching

Matthew 5-7

The Gospel by Matthew is the Gospel of the King and His kingdom. His *credentials* are presented in chapters 1-4, and the *constitution* of His kingdom is outlined in chapters 5-7. The Sermon on the Mount is a most important document. It has been called "the Manifesto of the Kingdom." It lays down the moral principles and laws by which the kingdom of heaven will be governed. Since the time of David and his brilliant reign over Israel, the theme of a coming kingdom ruled by the Messiah as King is a prominent theme of the Old Testament prophetic Scriptures. It is promised in the covenant given to David in 2 Samuel 7, and in the prophesies of Isaiah, Jeremiah, Ezekiel, and Daniel. Many of the psalms also predict the kingdom. In Matthew's Gospel alone it is called the Kingdom of Heaven.

The Sermon on the Mount is divided into three sections, with an introduction and a conclusion. The introduction (Matt. 5:1-12), gives a ninefold list of the moral attributes which should characterize the true citizens of the kingdom. They have been called Beattitudes, and each one is called blessed or happy. They have been compared to the ninefold fruit of the Spirit in Galatians 5:22-23. These true, loyal citizens are called "the salt of the earth" and "the light of the world" (vv. 13-16). They are to have a purifying and restraining influence on the corruption of earth and a bright vibrant testimony in a dark world. The main part of the section (vv. 17-47), refers to the moral laws of the kingdom. The Lord Jesus, who is the King, mentions a number of things which concern our public behavior. These are: murder, adultery, divorce, blasphemy, retaliation, and hatred. He compares these with the law of Mount Sinai. He emphasizes the fact that He has not come to destroy the law of Sinai but to fulfill it. He goes deeper, and exposes the hidden motives which cause these sins to be committed. These are the blatant sins of modern public life, and will be dealt with in swift justice when the King is on the throne. The section ends with the exhortation to the citizens: "Be ye therefore perfect, even as your Father which is in heaven is perfect." Obviously this does not mean to be sinless, but to maintain a sincere reaching after spiritual maturity.

The second section of the sermon (Matt. 6) deals with the inner, spiritual life of the citizen of the kingdom. Three features are mentioned: almsgiving, praying and fasting. A contrast is emphasized between the genuine and the counterfeit. Giving is to be done under God's eye and direction; praying is to be done in the secret place, is to be brief and sincere, following the example of the model prayer given by the King.

Fasting should be a deep spiritual exercise and not a public ritual to impress people. Then there are three warnings against covetousness, compromise, and anxious care about food and clothing. Our heavenly Father feeds the birds and adorns the lilies of the field. Will He not, then, take care of His dear children? The section closes with an important exhortation. "Seek ye first the Kingdom of God and His righteousness and all these things shall be added unto you." Nicodemus was reminded of this in John 3:7. It was imperative that he be born from above and transferred from the kingdom of darkness into the kingdom of God in order to obtain the righteousness of God which accompanied the transfer.

The third section of the Sermon on the Mount (Matt. 7) opened with a warning against hypocritical criticism of others, the critic proposing to remove the mote from his brother's eye while he has a block of wood in his own eye (vv. 1-5). Then follows an admonition not to offer precious pearls of teaching to the unclean, who would ignorantly reject it and trample it under their feet (v. 6). But God has precious blessing for those who ask and seek and knock at heaven's door (vv. 7-11). This is climaxed by the "Golden Rule" (v. 12). "Therefore all things whatsoever ye would that men should do to you, do ye so to them. For this is the law and the prophets." Love is the answer.

In verses 13-27, there is a series of contrasts between the true and the false: two gates, two roads, and two destinies—life and destruction (vv. 13-14); false prophets, two trees, and two fruits—good and bad (vv. 15-20); true and false profession (vv. 21-23); two builders, two houses, two foundations—rock or sand (vv. 24-27). In verses 28-29, we have the conclusion: two teachings—the King and the scribes. The people listened in astonishment, for the King spoke with authority and not as the scribes.

9
The Mount of Intercession

Matthew 14:23-33

Matthew's Gospel presents Jesus of Nazareth as the long-promised Messiah and King of Israel. On a mountaintop, the King outlined the principles of His kingdom in chapters 5-7. His forerunner, John the Baptist, preached repentance to the nation, as the kingdom was at hand. Chosen apostles were sent out announcing the Gospel of the kingdom. The King was authenticated by marvelous miracles and by an authoritative ministry.

But a crisis comes in chapter 12. The recognized leaders of Israel hold a council how they might destroy Him. The King and His kingdom are officially rejected. Their verdict is that His miracles and His ministry are satanically inspired. From that point on, the teaching of the kingdom takes a different form. Chapter 13 records the seven parables of the Kingdom of Heaven. The Kingdom is called a mystery. The rejected King will be mocked and crucified with a crown of thorns on His head. But He will rule from heaven in the hearts of His true followers. The seven parables describe conditions on the earth during His absence in heaven. One day He will come back in glory and will establish His kingdom in righteousness and peace.

Matthew 14 gives a panoramic picture of conditions subsequent to the rejection of the King. There are seven panels to the picture, with an introduction and an appendix. It comes between the parables of the Kingdom of Heaven in chapter 13, and the revelation of the Church in chapter 16.

1) *Herod's Birthday Feast* (vv. 1-14). It was the birthday of Herod Antipas, the son of Herod the Great, the man who murdered the children of Bethlehem (Matt. 2:16-18). He was living in adultery with Herodias, the wife of his brother Philip. John the Baptist had boldly rebuked him, saying, "It is not lawful for thee to have her." As a result, John was in prison. The birthday feast was a brilliant affair, with an august attendance. The daughter of Herodias danced and the pleased king, with an oath, promised to give her anything she desired, even to the half of his kingdom. Instructed by her mother, she asked for the head of John on a platter. The prison was near to the palace. An executioner performed the horrible task, presented the decapitated head to the girl, and she took it to her mother. Herodias had her revenge!

The whole scenario is a graphic picture of the godless world. No element is lacking: culture, entertainment, immorality, superstition, persecution.

Later, our Lord called Herod "that fox" (Lk. 13:32), and when He was brought before him by Pilate, He refused to cater to his curiosity or answer his questions. Herod and his men of war set Him at naught, and sent Him back to Pilate, in mockery dressed in a borrowed purple robe. The world today has not changed. The Herods of ancient times have many followers and imitators.

2) *Our Lord's Feast of Compassion* (vv. 13-21). When the disciples of John heard of his tragic death, they came and took his body and buried it; then went and told Jesus. We can imagine His feelings. John was His friend and forerunner who had announced His mission and His deity. In His sorrow, He wanted to get away and be alone. He got into a boat

and went to a desert place apart. But when the people heard of it, they followed Him on foot out of the cities. The subsequent story is told in all four Gospels. Seeing the hungry multitude as sheep without a shepherd, He was moved with compassion. He healed the sick among them, and then He fed them. The word, "compassion," is used seven times in the Gospels and of the Saviour alone. It means "to suffer together."

The miracle of the feeding of five thousand with five loaves and two fishes reminds us of the miracles of Elijah and Elisha. Mark mentions the detail that the disciples estimated that it would cost two hundred denarii to feed the crowd, that they were divided into ranks of hundreds and fifties, and that they sat upon the green grass. John introduces Philip and the lad who had the loaves and the fishes, and says they were barley loaves. Matthew, Mark, and John all testify that five thousand took part in the meal, that they were filled, and that there were twelve baskets of fragments left over. There is a very different and designed contrast between the murderous Herod's birthday party and the compassionate Christ feeding the hungry multitude. One represents the world, the other the gospel feast motivated by love and shepherd care.

3) *The Mount of Intercessory Prayer* (v. 23). "And straightway Jesus constrained His disciples to get into a ship, and to go before Him unto the other side, while He sent the multitudes away. And when He had sent the multitudes away, He went up into a mountain apart to pray; and when the evening was come, He was there alone." At last, He had the opportunity of being alone in the secret place of the Most High with His Father. This is one of three occasions when we are told our Lord spent the night in prayer. The other two are recorded in Luke 6:12 and John 7:53-8:1.

John 6:4 tells us that the Passover was near. The new moon would be shining. Here is a picture of our Lord today—on the throne as our Advocate, Intercessor, and High Priest. In His ascension ministry as our Advocate, He pleads for us when we sin (1 John 2:1); as our Intercessor, He is able to save us when we suffer (Heb. 7:25); and as our Great High Priest, He can sympathize with us in our sorrows and temptations (Heb. 2:18).

4) *The Ship in the Storm* (vv. 22-24). While He was on the mountaintop, the ship was "in the midst of the sea, tossed with waves for the wind was contrary." The lake was forty furlongs broad (8 miles). They had barely started when the storm broke, so they lowered the sail and took to the oars. They toiled in rowing, but in the middle of the lake they caught the full force of the gale. The wind roared down the glens on the shore and in nine hours they had only made three miles.

There are three things they might have done: (1) give up, turn back and run before the wind to the place they had left; (2) tack from side to side on a zig-zag course; (3) or keep their head to the wind and toil on. They had received their orders from the Master, and there was no turning back.

Noah at the flood, the Psalmist in Psalm 107, Jonah, Paul, and the Lord Himself—all had experienced the fury of the storm. Life is not always calm and peaceful, but thank God there is a bright hope as this beautiful narrative unfolds.

(5) *The Saviour Comes in the Fourth Watch of the Night* (vv. 25-27). "And in the fourth watch of the night, Jesus went unto them, walking on the sea. And when the disciples saw Him walking on the sea, they were troubled, saying, It is a spirit; and they cried out for fear. But straightway Jesus spoke unto them saying, Be of good cheer; it is I; be not afraid."

The Jews only observed three watches in the night, but the Romans had four: evening, midnight, cockcrow, and morning. The morning watch was 3-6 AM. It was reckoned to be the darkest, weakest, coldest, sleepiest watch of the night, just before the dawn. When Jesus came to the rescue of the storm-tossed disciples, He had the cause of their trouble beneath

His feet. They could not believe what they were seeing. They thought it must be a *phantasma* (Gk.) or an apparition (RV). These men had gallantly fought the tempest, but this unmanned them. In answer to their frightened cry, Jesus calmed them with six words (v. 27): "It is I, be not afraid." Peter responded, "Lord, if it be Thou, bid me come unto Thee on the water." Jesus said, "Come."

6) *Peter's Walk of Faith* (vv. 29-31). Only Matthew records that walk. The secret is the Lord's command, "Come." To act without it would have been presumption. For those in the boat, it was collective faith, but to walk on the water was individual faith. It reminds us of man's first walk in space, but there was the golden cord and lifeline of security. For Peter, it was one word from the Omnipotent Christ—the Master of wind and wave and circumstance. It reminds us, too, of George Muller, who trusted God to care for thousands of orphan children for more than fifty years, without making any appeal for funds. It also brings to mind the host of missionaries and other servants of the Lord who, at God's command, "stepped out into the seeming void and found the Rock beneath."

But seeing the wind boisterous, fear gripped Peter and, beginning to sink, he cried out, "Lord, save me." And immediately Jesus, having already put out His hand, caught him and said, "O thou of little faith, wherefore didst thou doubt?" Peter had his eye on the surroundings instead of on the Lord. Sometimes God allows His servant to reach the last penny or the last crust, and the agonizing brief prayer, but then the miracle of deliverance comes.

7) *Safe Arrival on Shore* (cf. Jn. 6:21). The disciples gladly received Him into the ship, and "immediately the ship was at the land whither they went." John implies a miracle. He imparted to the boat that victorious power over gravity and space as He had to Peter and His own Person. Matthew adds: "And when they were come into the ship, the wind ceased.

105

Then they that were in the ship came and worshipped Him, saying, Of a truth Thou art the Son of God."

Alexander MacLaren comments: "Those that have Christ for Captain will land on the eternal shore, and dry out their wet clothes in the sunshine."

10
The Mount of Transfiguration

Matthew 16:28-17:8

The Transfiguration of our Lord Jesus Christ is one of the most important of His earthly experiences. It is recorded in all the synoptic Gospels, and probably referred to in John 1:14. Peter expounds its meaning in his second epistle (1:13-19). Matthew places it between the first two mentions of the cross in his Gospel (16:21 and 17:23).

The Time: The section properly begins at chapter 16:21. "From that time forth began Jesus to show unto His disciples how that He must go unto Jerusalem, and suffer many things of the elders and chief priests and scribes, and be killed, and be raised again the third day." It was a time of crisis. Luke 9:51 shows that it was from this time that He started His journey to the cross. Notice that Matthew 16:27-28 is important as an introduction to the Transfiguration in chapter 17: "For the Son of Man shall come in the glory of His Father, with His angels; and then He shall reward every man according to his works. Verily I say unto you, There be some standing here, which shall not taste of death, till they see the Son of Man coming in His kingdom. And after six days, Jesus taketh Peter, James and John his brother, and bringeth them up into a high mountain apart." It is obvious that the Transfiguration scene is a preview of the coming of Christ in glory, as given here to certain selected witnesses.

The Place: It was a high mountain. It could not be the traditional Tabor in the heart of the Jezreel Valley. Josephus tells us that at this time, Tabor was crowned with a fortress at its crest. More likely, this high mountain was one of the slopes of Mount Hermon. Hermon is 9,400 feet in altitude, 11,000 feet above the Jordan Valley floor. Its snowy peak is so high that it can actually be seen on a clear day from the heights flanking the Dead Sea, over 100 miles away. It is only 14 miles from Caesarea Philippi where the events recorded in Matthew 16 took place.

Transfiguration: Luke 9:28-29 says that Jesus went up to the mountain to pray. It was as He prayed that the fashion of His countenance was altered (*heteron*) and His raiment became white and glistering. Matthew states that when He was transfigured before them, His face shone as the sun and His raiment was white as the light. The word "transfigured" is *metamorphothe* (*meta*—change, *morphe*—form).

The word is only used four times in the New Testament (Matt. 17:2; Mk. 9:2; Rom. 12:2; 2 Cor. 3:18). The word literally means "a change of form." The first two references are applied to the unique experience of our Lord. Philippians 2 informs us that He ever subsisted in the form of God, and in His humanity He took upon Him the form (*morphe*) of a servant. The glory of His Godhead was there, but it was a covered glory, veiled (Heb. 10:20) by the body of a Bondservant. On the mountaintop, He was transfigured, the inner glory of His Godhead shone out. It was not a reflected glory from outside, but the essential glory of His divine Person. The other two references in Romans and 2 Corinthians are translated "transformed" or "changed." They refer to the work of the Holy Spirit in the life of the believer, through the powerful influence of the Word, in conforming him more and more into the image of God's beloved Son.

Two Celestial Witnesses: These two witnesses, Moses and Elijah, appear on the last page of the Old Testament. Possibly, they are the witnesses of Revelation 11, representing the law and the prophets. Moses had been in the grave for 1,400 years (cf. Jude v. 9). Elijah had been raptured to heaven 900 years later. Here they appear with Christ in glory. They are a picture of heavenly saints raised at the Rapture, and reigning with Christ over the Millennial earth. Here the topic of their conversation with the Lord was His decease (Gk. *exodos*) which He should accomplish at Jerusalem (Lk. 9:31). This is the term used by Peter of his own death (2 Pet. 1:15). The word means "outgoing" (from *ex*—out, *hodos*—a way). Moses and Elijah had an exodus. The Lord calls His death a baptism (Lk. 12:50), but these heavenly saints had an exodus. It includes the ideas not only of death, but of resurrection and ascension. Their presence here is a pledge of immortality, for they were conscious beyond the grave. As well, the permanence of personality was recognized by the apostles. We shall know each other in heaven.

Three Earthly Witnesses: Peter, James and John, the inner circle of the apostles, were chosen to see the Lord raise a child from the dead (Mk. 5:37); to behold His glory on the mountaintop and His agony in the Garden of Gethsemane (Mk. 14:33). But on the last two occasions, they were fast asleep. They are a picture of Israel today, spiritually asleep to the agony and glory of their Messiah. But one day they will awake (Zech. 12:10). Luke tells us that Peter and the others were heavy with sleep, but when they awoke and saw the glory and the two heavenly witnesses about to leave, Peter said, "Lord, it is good to be here; let us make three tabernacles, one for Thee, and one for Moses, and one for Elias," not knowing what he said. Mark comments, "For he wist not what to say," because they were afraid. It is one of Peter's sad blunders. He put the Lord on the same level as His servants. His only excuse is that he was afraid and not properly awake. He was, however, immediately corrected.

The Bright Cloud and the Voice from Heaven: "This is My beloved Son, in whom I am well pleased," said the Voice. "Hear *Him*." The Voice from the cloud was previously declared in three messianic Scriptures: Psalm 2:7; Isaiah 42:1; and Deuteronomy 18:15. The first declares His Eternal Sonship, the second expounds the Person and work of the suffering Servant of Jehovah, and the third describes the Prophet sent from God to whom we must listen, not to fallible man. The bright cloud from which the divine Voice came was likely the Shekinah glory, manifesting the presence of God Himself. It was seen at the Ascension (Acts 1:9), and will be seen again at His coming in glory (Rev. 1:7).

The Meaning of the Transfiguration: The Lord tells us that the Transfiguration is a preview of the Son of Man coming in His kingdom (Matt. 16:28). Peter (2 Pet. 1:13-19) gives a number of reasons:

1) It is a picture of the power and coming of our Lord Jesus Christ. They were "eyewitnesses of His majesty." God gave them evidence for their eyes and ears, that they had not followed a cleverly concocted fable (v. 16).

2) The prophetic Word was made more sure (v. 19). The prophetic lamp was shining in a dark (a squalid, murky) place. The vision and the voice out of the cloud authenticated Christ as the Son and the Messiah.

3) The Transfiguration showed the relationship between the Cross and the Coming. The disciples were looking for an immediate earthly kingdom. This event was to set their thinking straight. First came the suffering, then came the glory. The cross must be borne before the crown would be worn. The face that shone as the sun would be spit upon; the garments that shone as the light, would be gambled for. Instead of the Voice from heaven, there would be the awful silence. The place of Moses and Elijah on either side would be taken by two thieves. But the glory and majesty of His reign as King

of Kings was assured. They had seen it with their own eyes!

4) This drama on the mountaintop had provided evidence of resurrection and immortality as well. They had seen two well-known historical figures, recognizable and able to communicate.

5) The Transfiguration also has a very practical application to us. This is the Blessed Hope. We shall be changed! Not only will we be with Him, we shall be like Him in that day.

11
The Mount of Prophecy

Matthew 24-25

In the last week of our Lord's ministry before the cross, He gave two great discourses to selected audiences. The first was on Mount Olivet to Peter, James, John, and Andrew. They represent the godly remnant of the nation of Israel. The second discourse was in the Upper Room in Jerusalem to a gathering of all the apostles. They were the nucleus of what was later to be the Church. The subject of the first concerned the prophetic future; the theme of the second was a devotional outline of the fundamentals of Christianity, concluding with a farewell prayer.

Jesus had been rejected by the nation of Israel. On leaving the temple—the central shrine—for the last time, someone enthused on its beauty and majesty. To that, Jesus sadly remarked: "Truly I say unto you, there shall not be left here one stone upon another which shall not be thrown down." Later, at a private interview, as He sat on the Mount of Olives, Peter, James, John, and Andrew asked Him two questions:

1) *When* shall these things be?

2) *What* shall be the sign of Thy coming and of the end of the world (age)?

As the two questions refer to two separate historical

events, the Lord answered them separately. Luke alone in his Gospel (21:20-24) records the details of the answer given by the Lord to the first question: "And when ye shall see Jerusalem encompassed with armies, then know that the desolation thereof is nigh . . . And they shall fall by the edge of the sword, and shall be led away captive into all nations: and Jerusalem shall be trodden down of the Gentiles until the times of the Gentiles be fulfilled" (v. 24). This happened in AD 70 when the Roman armies invaded the land, destroyed the temple, and levelled the city. Josephus, the Jewish historian, tells us that more than a million Jews perished and that at least 97,000 were captured. An attempted rebellion of the remnant in AD 134 was ruthlessly smashed, and this time the foundations of the city were plowed up. The Lord's prediction concerning the destruction of the temple and the city was literally fulfilled.

It is Matthew (chs. 24-25) that gives us the answer to the second question, "What shall be the sign of Thy coming, and of the end of the world (age)?" The Lord's reply is in three parts: the coming in relation to Israel; three parables relating to the time of the Lord's absence; and the coming in relation to the judgment of the living Gentile nations.

THE COMING IN RELATION TO ISRAEL (MATT. 24:4-44)

It is obvious that the coming of the Son of Man in this context is not the Rapture, which had not yet been revealed. Note seven terms in the passage: temple, Holy Place, Judea, Sabbath day, Gospel of the Kingdom, tribes of the land, the Great Tribulation. The events described here take place after the Chuch is raptured.

This section is in four parts, with a final exhortation.

1) *The Beginning of Sorrows* (vv. 4-14). This describes the first 3 years and 6 months after the Rapture. It parallels the four horsemen of Revelation 6. A warning of deception is mentioned four times. At this point, God will call and send

forth 144,000 Jewish witnesses to preach the Gospel of the Kingdom to the whole world.

2) *The Great Tribulation* (vv. 15-26). This embraces the last 3 years and 6 months. It commences with the Abomination of Desolation being set up in the Holy Place of a rebuilt temple in Jerusalem (2 Thess. 2:3-12). This period will see the rise of an unholy trinity, the two beasts of Revelation 13, energized by Satan. During this awful time, the vials (bowls) of Revelation 15-16 will be poured out.

3) *The Coming of the Son of Man* (vv. 27-39). The Apocalypse, the coming in glory of the once-despised Nazarene, will draw out the united fury of the nations. They will gather at Armageddon (Zech. 12-14). See also Revelation 1:7; 19:1-21.

4) *The Four Signs* (vv. 29-39). Here now is the answer to the second question, What shall be the sign of Thy coming? The Lord Jesus gives them four signs: There is the Celestial Sign. The sun and moon will be darkened and stars will fall from heaven (v. 29). There is the National Sign—the blossoming of the fig tree (vv. 32-33; Matt. 21:18-20; Luke 13:6-9). He gives a Chronological Sign (v. 34), that this generation shall not pass till all these things be fulfilled. Finally, there is a Moral and Social Sign—the world will behave as they did in the days of Noah (vv. 37-38). This section ends with a final exhortation. The Lord portrays two men working in the field, when one is suddenly taken, and the other is left. Two women will be grinding at the mill; one will be taken, the other left. It is to be noted that the one taken is taken away in judgment, the other is left for kingdom blessing. Matthew records the warning to watch. Mark calls men to pray. Luke joins the two: watch and pray.

THREE KINGDOM PARABLES (MATT. 24:45-25:30)

Here are described the moral conditions during the absence of the King. Three tests are given in view of the Lord's coming. There is a vital link with this passage and the seven parables of the kingdom of heaven in Matthew 13. (The exposition by William Kelly is helpful here.)

1) The contrast between the wise and evil servants presents the test of *fidelity* (24:45-51).

2) The contrast between the wise and foolish virgins shows the test of *reality* (25:1-13).

3) The contrast between the faithful and false stewards emphasizes the test of *activity* (25:14-30).

JUDGMENT OF THE LIVING NATIONS (MATT. 25:31-46)

The *occasion* of this judgment is given in verse 31—when the Son of Man comes in His glory. The *place* (v. 32) is The Valley of Jehoshaphat, which means decision or concision (see Joel 3:14; Zech. 14:1-3). The Church will be present at it (1 Cor. 6:2).

The *judged* (v. 32) are all the nations—the survivors after the judgments of Revelation 6-19. It will also include unbelieving Israel, and every follower of the Beast and Antichrist. The *basis* of judgment will be the reception or rejection of the Gospel of the Kingdom proclaimed by those the Lord refers to as "My brethren"—the 144,000 of Revelation 7 and 14.

This judgment will be the separation of the sheep and goats. Sheep are those who are permitted to go into the kingdom for earthly blessing. The goats are rejecters who are cast into eternal fire. (Cf. the dragnet judgment of Matt. 13:47-48.)

12
Mount Calvary

Matthew 27

Each of the four Gospels gives a detailed account of the crucifixion and death of the Saviour. Matthew is the Gospel of the King-Messiah. His emphasis is on the supernatural. Matthew underscores the miraculous virgin birth, and in chapters 8-9, he describes ten miracles performed by Jesus in the four spheres of disease, demon possession, death, and His power over natural forces. In the middle of this series of wonder-working, he tells of his own conversion, with the implication that this too was a miracle. It all authenticated the fact that Jesus of Nazareth was the Son of God, sent by the Father, and the King-Messiah of Old Testament prophecy.

The first mention of the sufferings and death of Christ in Matthew's Gospel is in chapter 16:21. He had been officially rejected by the Jewish government in chapter 12. In chapter 16:18, the Lord announced the building of His Church, and immediately after He revealed that He was going to suffer and die at Jerusalem, but would be resurrected on the third day. From that point (16:21) to chapter 26:26, His death is mentioned ten times in the narrative. Matthew calls the site of execution, Golgotha, the place of a skull. He speaks of the narcotic to deaden the pain, vinegar mingled with gall—

which our Lord refused—of the gambling for His garments, and of the fact that the soldiers sat down and watched Him there. It is recorded that the placard above His head was written in three languages: THIS IS JESUS, THE KING OF THE JEWS. The record tells of a threefold mockery of the dying Saviour: by the thieves crucified with Him, by the passers-by, and by the religious leaders who sarcastically quoted Scripture. The other Gospels mention the four times that Jesus spoke during the three hours of daylight from 9 AM until noon; His prayer to His Father for forgiveness for those who had crucified Him, the promise to the repentant dying thief, the word of compassion to His mother and the committal of His mother to the care of the apostle John. Then at high noon we have described the first of the five miracles at the cross:

1) From the sixth to the ninth hour there was darkness over the whole land (v. 45). Luke 23:45 says, "The sun was darkened" (passive). It was an act of Almighty God. It was not just an ordinary eclipse of the sun which lasts for 15 minutes. This lasted for three hours. Scripture speaks of three periods of darkness: primeval darkness (Gen. 1:2); the Egyptian plague of darkness (Ex. 10:21); and the horror of outer darkness (Matt. 22:13). All three speak of judgment.

What, then, is the meaning of the darkness which enshrouded Golgotha? Here we approach with holy reverence and unshod feet. "And about the ninth hour (3 PM, the time of the evening sacrifice) Jesus cried with a loud voice, Eli, Eli, lama sabachthani, My God, My God, why hast Thou forsaken Me?" This is the reason for the darkness. It was a solitary transaction between a holy God and His beloved Son. It was the supreme moment of time, the meeting place between two eternities, when Jehovah laid upon Him the iniquities of us all. Here was the accomplishment of the vicarious atonement. It was for the whole world, for you and for me.

2) "Jesus when He had cried again with a loud voice, yielded up the ghost." The unique character of the death of Christ

is indicated by the word used by both Matthew and John when He died. "Yielded up" is *aphiemi*, to send away. We are reminded of His words in John 10:17-18. Speaking as the Good Shepherd, He said: "Therefore doth My Father love Me because I lay down My life that I may take it again. No man taketh it from Me, but I lay it down of Myself. I have power to lay it down, and I have power to take it again. This commandment have I received of My Father." When He cried with the triumphant shout, "It is finished," the sacrificial work was done and He added, "Father, into Thy hands I commend My spirit," and He bowed His head and released His spirit. His death was voluntary, vicarious, and victorious.

3) Simultaneous with the death of Christ, another significant miracle took place. The veil of the temple was torn in two from the top to the bottom. This veil, a beautiful piece of tapestry, is described in Exodus 26:31-33. Its colors were of blue, purple, scarlet, and fine twined linen, with pictures of cherubim woven into the fabric. It was held up by four pillars of wood overlaid with gold standing in sockets of silver. In the sanctuary, it divided the holy place from the inner shrine, the holiest of all. Only the high priest was permitted to enter the holiest once a year on the Day of Atonement. For any unauthorized person to enter beyond the veil meant death. Hebrews 10:20 tells us that the veil is a type of the body (flesh) of our Lord. By His holy body being torn on the cross and His blood being shed, we now have access into the immediate presence of God. It is interesting to note that this miracle took place at the time of the evening sacrifice and the functioning priest must have been aware of it. Perhaps this is the reason we read that later a great company of the priests were obedient to the faith (Acts 6:7).

4) There was also an earthquake. At the death (v. 51) and the resurrection of Christ there was an earthquake (28:2). As well, at His coming again in glory, "His feet shall stand . . . upon the Mount of Olives . . . and the mount shall cleave in

the midst . . . and there shall be a very great valley; and half of the mountain shall remove toward the north, and half of it toward the south . . . And it shall be in that day, that living waters shall go out from Jerusalem, half of them toward the former sea, (Mediteranean) and half of them toward the hinder sea (the Dead Sea). In summer and winter shall it be" (Zech. 14:4, 8). The Lord predicted that in the latter times there would be famines and pestilences and earthquakes in various places (Matt. 24:7). Recent events in the world scene surely point to that time.

5) The fifth miracle is described in the words, "And the graves were opened; and many bodies of the saints which slept arose, and came out of the graves after His resurrection, and went into the holy city, and appeared unto many" (vv. 52-53). Only Matthew records this event. Note the following: First, there was a selection—it states that many, not all sleeping saints arose. Second, they were saints, genuine believers. Third, it was a bodily resurrection. Fourth, they arose *after* His resurrection. He was the Firstfruits of resurrection and the First-begotten from the dead. Fifth, it was a real resurrection, not a resuscitation, like Lazarus and the widow of Nain's son who obviously later died and went back to the grave. The fact that these saints went into the holy city and appeared to many would be witness to the truth of the bodily resurrection of Christ and to that of the believer. As the Scriptures do not describe what happened to these saints after their resurrection and appearance in Jerusalem, any comment would be mere speculation. We shall know when we reach the heavenly shore.

It is obvious that in Matthew's account of the death of our Lord Jesus Christ, he emphasizes the supernatural element in the five miracles which he records. But it is climaxed by the super-miracle of His resurrection described in chapter 28. "In the end of the sabbath, as it began to dawn towards the first day of the week, came Mary Magdalene and the other Mary to see the sepulchre. And, behold, there was a great earthquake; for the angel of the Lord descended from heaven, and came and rolled back the stone from the door, and sat upon it. His countenance was like lightning, and his raiment white as snow. And for fear of him the keepers did shake, and became as dead men. And the angel answered and said unto the women, "Fear not ye, for I know that ye seek Jesus which was crucified. He is not here; for He is risen, as He said. Come, see the place where the Lord lay."

The vicarious, atoning death of the Lord Jesus, His burial, and the miracle of His bodily resurrection, is the foundation of Christianity and the subject of the Gospel.

13
The Mountain in Galilee

Matthew 28

The great commission to take the message of salvation to the world is emphasized in all four Gospels, but it was given in different locations and wording. That in Matthew is the first and fullest. The place was to be a mountain in Galilee. It is mentioned three times, showing its importance. First, it was stated by our Lord Himself before His crucifixion: "But after I am risen again, I will go before you into Galilee" (Matt. 26:32). It was reiterated by the angel of the Lord to the women at the sepulchre on the resurrection morning (Matt. 28:7). Then the eleven disciples went away into Galilee, to a mountain where Jesus had appointed them (v. 16). There seems to be three reasons for the importance of the meeting in Galilee. First, it is the only one prearranged three times. Second, (if it is the same meeting mentioned in 1 Corinthians 15:6) for the great number present—the passage says 500. Third, it was the occasion of the most official commission. There is a very close link between two appearings of the Lord Jesus in His post-resurrection ministry. At the lakeshore in John 21, the disciples were taught the lessons of catching fish and feeding sheep. On the mountaintop, they were given the command and the vital principles of taking the Gospel to the whole world. But why Galilee of the Gentiles and not Jerusalem of the chosen people? The answer is simple: the King had been rejected by Israel and now the Gospel is to be preached to the whole world.

THE GREAT COMMISSION (MATT. 28:18-20).

The passage opens with the revelation of divine Omnipotence in terrrestrial (the earthquake) and celestial (the angelic appearance) spheres. It closes with Omniscience and Omnipresence—not only does He fill all space with His authority, but all time with His presence. Matthew opens with Emmanuel—God with us—and closes with the divine title, I AM: "I AM with you alway."

The teaching swings around three co-terminus phrases: all nations; all things commanded; and all the days. This underscores the totality of the territory to be reached; the totality of the teaching to be given; and the totality of the time in which the Lord will give His servants aid. He will not abandon us at the end of the age.

Notice the five great themes woven together here:

1) *Lordship:* "All authority." This is the word *exousia,* not *dunamis,* although the latter (power) is also true. Heaven and earth submit to His sway. What a claim! What did the devil think of it? He had offered the kingdoms of this world and the glory of them to our Lord at His temptation. But the risen Christ, who conquered Satan at the Cross, can claim all authority and power in heaven and on earth. No head of state, king, or president can make a claim like this today. In human hands power corrupts, but He is King of kings and Lord of lords. His rule is characterized by perfect wisdom, love, and power. We welcome His Kingship and bow to His Lordship. But is He practically Lord of our hearts, homes, assemblies, and in the great work of the harvestfield?

2) *Discipleship:* "Make disciples." In Mark 16:15, the commission is "Go ye . . . and preach" (*keruso*). Here it is the

word disciple (*matheieuo*). Holy Ghost preaching should result in believers accepting the message, but discipleship goes a step farther. A disciple is a convert consecrated—a follower, a learner. The only other place where the word is used is Acts 14:21. Towards the end of their first missionary journey, Paul and Barnabas came to Derbe, "And when they had preached the Gospel to that city, and had taught many, they returned again to Lystra and Iconium and Antioch, confirming the souls of the disciples, and exhorting them to continue in the faith, and that we must with much tribulation enter into the kingdom of God. And when they had ordained them elders in every church, and had prayed with fasting, they commended them to the Lord on whom they believed." These verses outline the seven steps in the discipling of believers.

3) *Fellowship:* "Baptizing them into the Name." This is not John's baptism of repentance, nor the baptism in the Holy Spirit into one Body which took place at Pentecost, but the water baptism of believers who accept the Gospel and are born again during the present church dispensation. On confession of their faith, the full formula is used by the person performing the baptism. It is "into (*eis*) the name of the Father, and of the Son, and of the Holy Spirit." Although in the Acts of the Apostles we read of baptism being performed in the name of Jesus Christ (Acts 2:38), into the name of the Lord Jesus (Acts 8:16), and in the name of the Lord (Acts 10:48), it does not abrocate the use of the complete formula. It simply means that it was carried out by the authority or command of the Lord Jesus. It was He who ordered it and we must be careful to go back to the original terms of the command. The beautiful symbol of baptism illustrates the death, burial, and resurrection of the Saviour. All three members of the Holy Trinity were involved in each of these great events, and we are called upon to publicly identify ourselves with this.

4) *Apprenticeship:* "Teaching them to observe all things . . . I have commanded." This is God's school. The work of the

125

evangelist, the shepherd, and the teacher is needed (Eph. 4:7-13; 2 Tim. 4:1-5). The evangelist specifically has a threefold responsibility: evangelizing, baptizing, and teaching the converts. Follow-up is important.

Paul told the elders at Ephesus that he had preached all the counsel of God and kept back nothing that was profitable (Acts 20:20). He had not compromised the truth, but had worked, and warned, and wept with concern for their spiritual well-being. This is an eloquent example for all true servants of God.

5) *Companionship:* "Lo, I am with you alway, even to the end of the age." Note the connection between "Go" and "Lo." It has been said that the shortest distance between two points is a good companion. Here we have the promise of the Lord Himself to be with the servant who obeys the command to go. The history of missionary work since Pentecostal days is a thrilling one, but is not yet complete. Millions have obeyed the call to go, and have claimed the promise of the Presence. Many are still on the front lines of the battle and we are nearing the end of the age. It is a difficult and dangerous day, but we remember the witness of David Livingstone. When surrounded by hostile tribes, he read the promise, "Lo, I am with you always," and wrote in his diary, "These are the words of a Perfect Gentleman, and can be trusted as such."

Part Three
Epilogue

In these pages we have been tracing the records of six men in the Old Testament—Noah, Abraham, Moses, Caleb, David, and Elijah—who had an experience with God on a mountaintop. Each summit crisis changed their lives and their appreciation of the wisdom and power of Almighty God. They also had valley experiences which balanced the euphoria of the heights.

Then in the New Testament, in Matthew's Gospel, we see our Lord seven times on a mountain, linked with important and precious truths: His temptation by Satan (ch. 4:8); the Sermon on the Mount (chs. 5-7); the Mount of Prayer (ch.14:23); the Mount of Transfiguration (ch. 17:1); the Mount of Prophecy (chs. 24-25); Mount Calvary (ch. 27); and the Mountain in Galilee (ch. 28:16). Our Lord also had deep valley experiences, but was triumphant at the last.

It is significant that John the Apostle, at the end of the book of the Revelation, is carried away in the spirit to a great and high mountain to get a vision of the home of the Bride, the Lamb's wife (Rev. 21:10). At the beginning of the book, he falls at the feet of the risen Christ and there he gets a message for each of the seven churches of Asia Minor (chs. 2-3). But after the Rapture of the Church and the sad details of the Great Tribulation and the judgment of the counterfeit church, he is taken to the mountaintop to get a panoramic view of the Holy City and the new heavens and earth. What a glorious climax!

> When we reach our peaceful dwelling
> On the strong, eternal hills,
> And our praise to Him is swelling,
> Who the vast creation fills—
> When the paths of prayer and duty
> And affliction all are trod,
> And we wake to see the beauty
> Of our Saviour and our God:
> Oh! 'twill be a glorious morrow
> To a dark and stormy day,
> When we smile upon our sorrow,
> And the storms have passed away.
> —W. P. Mackay